The Final Exam
Letters to Our Students

MAGGID

Rabbi Dr. Ari Berman

THE
FINAL EXAM
Letters to Our Students

Yeshiva University Press
Maggid Books

The Final Exam
Letters to Our Students

First edition, 2023

Maggid Books
An imprint of Koren Publishers Jerusalem Ltd.

PO Box 8531, New Milford, CT 06776-8531, USA
& PO Box 4044, Jerusalem 9104001, Israel
www.korenpub.com

Hardcover ISBN: 978-1-59264-623-4

Printed and bound in Turkey

Dedicated in honor of

Rabbi Dr. Ari Berman

Thank you for making Yeshiva University the flagship Jewish university through your erudition, vision, and leadership.

Debbie and Elliot Gibber

To my wife, Anita,
and our children
Shlomo
Yehuda
Binyamin
Tamar
and
Yonatan
whose love and devotion to me, to each other,
and to the great Jewish story
have made all this possible

Contents

Introduction

My Dear Student,

Over the past few years, I have been traveling from campus to campus, state to state, and country to country learning about the extraordinary reach of Yeshiva University and taking pride in our students, graduates, faculty, staff, and lay leaders.

In my years here, Yeshiva University was invited to represent one branch of the menorah at the Kotel for Israel's national lighting ceremony. Yeshiva University was represented in Dubai at the first ever Holocaust commemoration day in an Arab country. Yeshiva University has hosted global leaders and thinkers at public events on our campuses. On every one of these significant occasions, I came away recognizing that people the world over regard Yeshiva University as the flagship Jewish university.

In fact, at no time in its history has this institution of higher learning been more important or more necessary. In a sea of relativism, cancel culture, and harsh political discourse, our Yeshiva University is holding firmly to tradition in its confrontation with and integration of modernity. חַדֵּשׁ יָמֵינוּ כְּקֶדֶם, "Renew our days as of old" (*Eicha* 5:21). We take the best of the past, and it informs our present and our future. We grow, learn, and discover. We experiment, innovate, and approach the world with a posture of curiosity *and* with the anchor of our history, rooted in our commitment to Halacha.

In this relatively new century, as an institution that is itself older than a century, we need a current exposition of our educational philosophy and worldview that speaks to the wholeness of each individual student as well as the depth of our multi-millennial tradition.

Ironically, while many beyond our walls recognize what is unique and invaluable in our YU schools and communities, at times our students within them have trouble articulating our distinct outlook. It is instinctively obvious to our Yeshiva University family that we represent an outlook on life that is both timely and timeless, but we ourselves may struggle for the language to define it, to verbalize it, and to communicate it.

This inability can sometimes cause confusion, misunderstanding, and even defection. While for generations there was a sense that YU's values could be absorbed through osmosis by simply studying a dual curriculum and living on campus, experience has borne out the importance of explicitly spelling out our priorities.

That is what this book aims to do. It demonstrates that our voice matters. And your voice matters.

I chose to tell the story of my journey at Yeshiva University and my desire to express its worldview through the form of letters. Letters communicate ideas in a more intimate and personal way. I began writing letters to students during Covid as a way to keep in touch despite the isolation. Letter-writing as a form of teaching is not new. In 1838, at the age of twenty-eight, Rabbi Samson Raphael Hirsch wrote his influential *Nineteen Letters on Judaism* as a fictional correspondence to a young intellectual who questioned the relevance of traditional Judaism. In his *Nineteen Letters*, Rabbi Hirsch wrote that the Torah is "noble and sublime" and is able to respond to all modern challenges and developments. It was Rabbi Hirsch who popularized the expression "*Torah im derech eretz,*" which has been translated and understood in a variety of ways, from "Torah with the integration of culture" to "Torah in combination with society's mores or norms."

I am, of course, no Rabbi Hirsch. But two centuries later, I humbly offer my own nineteen letters to you, our students, to help you consider how you can maximize these next years of your life, which will be some of the most significant in your own personal development.

Warmly,
Ari Berman

Letter #1

Your Final Exam

My Dear Student,

I hope this letter finds you well.

Indeed, your well-being is the whole reason I am here in the first place.

Allow me to explain.

At the end of our lives, the Talmud teaches us that there is a final exam (Shabbat 31a).

אָמַר רָבָא: בְּשָׁעָה שֶׁמַּכְנִיסִין אָדָם לְדִין, אוֹמְרִים לוֹ: נָשָׂאתָ וְנָתַתָּ בֶּאֱמוּנָה? קָבַעְתָּ עִתִּים לַתּוֹרָה? עָסַקְתָּ בִּפְרִיָּה וּרְבִיָּה? צָפִיתָ לִישׁוּעָה? פִּלְפַּלְתָּ בְּחָכְמָה? הֵבַנְתָּ דָּבָר מִתּוֹךְ דָּבָר?

Rava said: After departing from this world, when a person is brought to judgment for the life he lived in this world, they say to him:

1. Did you conduct business faithfully?
2. Did you designate times for Torah study?

1

3. Did you engage in procreation?
4. Did you anticipate the redemption?
5. Did you engage in the dialectics of wisdom?
6. Did you understand one matter from another?

In the fullness of time, we will each stand before God. We will be asked questions about how we spent our time here in this world. Collectively, the answers to these questions express the way in which we lived, worked, loved, studied, and built a better tomorrow. They challenge us and guide us at crossroads in our lives and in our day-to-day decisions. From Rava's perspective, all of our education and years on earth are a preparation for this final exam.

As someone who has devoted years of my life in high school, yeshiva, and university settings, I am only too familiar with final exams. Studying for days and sometime weeks, taking notes and summarizing the material, are all ways I prepare. But imagine if someone gave you the questions ahead of time. You received a brief study guide that laid out with perfect clarity what it was you were expected to answer. And part of that study guide included an easy to remember system to help you keep the core concepts in mind. How valuable would that study guide be to you?

In my mind, our education at Yeshiva University uniquely prepares you – and me – for this final exam, and in that context this book is like a study guide to help you understand the purpose of a YU education.

For the past several years, I have thought deeply about the right language to communicate Yeshiva University's unique approach to education and authentic Jewish living. I walked our halls, spoke with our students, met with parents, trustees, donors, friends, and alumni, conferred with our deans, faculty, and Jewish thought leaders, and worked with our esteemed rabbis, educators, and senior *Roshei Yeshiva*. Based on my own studies at YU and these conversations, I formulated a shorthand way to frame our education – our five core Torah values – as a vehicle to express and transmit our comprehensive worldview, to help us prepare for this final test in order that we live a life of love, learning, and service.

It is essential that we focus on Rava's questions and our core values at Yeshiva University today.

Our basic priority is clear. We are here in this world to serve God. רֵאשִׁית חׇכְמָה יִרְאַת ה', "The beginning of wisdom is to revere God" (*Tehillim* 111:10), and סוֹף דָּבָר הַכֹּל נִשְׁמָע אֶת הָאֱלֹקִים יְרָא וְאֶת מִצְוֹתָיו שְׁמוֹר, "The end of the matter is to revere God and observe the *mitzvot*" (*Kohelet* 12:14). From beginning to end, our task is to revere God and observe God's commandments. In fact, Rava ends his question list by telling us that the entire purpose of these retrospective questions is to create a life of *yirat Hashem*, reverence for God.

Initially, it seems pretty simple, but from here the questions become more difficult and demanding. What does a life of serving and fearing God look like? What is it that God wants from us? How do we identify that and how do we get there?

On the following pages, I will introduce you to some of the architects and leaders whose guiding principles made YU what it is today, and I will also share a new framework with which to consider a YU education. In my mind, our five core Torah values are not simply a conceptualization of foundational principles of Jewish life; they are a basis on which every student – and every person – can live a life of profound Jewish significance. I have included both Hebrew texts and their translations to address all those in our diverse student body, and I have included sources as an index in the back of the book for those who would like to study and discuss the material more fully. I have presented a theoretical framework with only some applications within our own educational system. I resist the temptation to make all of this practical for you, since that is your life's work and mine. Only you can take these core values and apply them to your *unique* life in your *unique* way because no one else can take this final exam for you.

Our worldview and educational philosophy are critical not only for our institution, but for all people who look to tradition as their bedrock of meaning and purpose. As people move both to the left and to the right, seeking either what they perceive as greater progressivism or greater conservatism, more inclusion or less, we have suffered from an attenuated and sometimes impoverished view of what Torah Judaism can contribute to our lives and to the world. I believe our five Torah values speak directly to the context of our times. From the days of the Talmud onward, sages and rabbis, educators and lay leaders have worked to formulate guiding principles for those looking to fulfill the Torah mandate to pursue a life of piety while also studying, working, raising a family, and making contributions to society.

To be clear, there is nothing exceptionally new in this presentation. Nothing about our core Torah values is new at all. That, in fact, is the point. This formulation is primarily a distillation of the thought of our revered teacher, Rabbi Joseph Soloveitchik, who articulated a worldview that emerges from a deep study and understanding of our Torah texts and rabbinic tradition dating back to Sinai. There is only one Torah and 613 Torah commandments. The five core Torah values help us live lives steeped in the Torah's wisdom while embracing modernity and its challenges through a compelling, multi-valenced prism. The core values honor Torah U-Madda as an educational philosophy while expanding it into a worldview that also embraces truth, dignity, and compassion. They inspire us to integrate these values into a meaningful life of religious integrity that sets as its goal a path to redemption.

Most importantly, as you begin on this path, I offer you the greatest blessing of all: May you feel that Hashem is with you throughout your journey here and beyond. By feeling Hashem's presence, you will never be alone; you will always be loved and always comforted, and you will always walk through life supported and strengthened.

חִזְקוּ וְאִמְצוּ... כִּי ה' אֱלֹקֶיךָ הוּא הַהֹלֵךְ עִמָּךְ לֹא יַרְפְּךָ וְלֹא יַעַזְבֶךָּ.

Be strong and courageous...for the Lord your God goes with you; He will never leave you nor forsake you. (*Devarim* 31:6)

Let's study hard for this final exam that earns the most important grade: the fulfillment of our life's purpose.

B'vracha,
Ari Berman

Letter #2

Welcome to Our Family

My Dear Student,

Welcome to our YU family. I am delighted that you are here, and I am committed to helping you prepare for this life test.

Our family is guided by a motto – Torah U-Madda – that appears on our family crest. Torah U-Madda is an educational philosophy that prioritizes Torah while simultaneously recognizing the religious value of worldly wisdom. We combine the best of Torah study and practice with a rigorous academic education to give you a spiritual, intellectual, and professional foundation. But we understand that to integrate these realms well and authentically requires a more comprehensive and holistic approach to your education and to your religious life. After much discussion, I have distilled the prism by which we accomplish our motto and lead lives of meaning, purpose, and service into the five core Torah values. The mere act of studying both domains will not alone enable us to pass Hashem's final exam. Life is larger than any motto could ever be.

As we begin this journey together, I want to share these values and how they inspire us to formulate our own answers to Rava's questions.

1. **Torat Emet** (Seek Truth): We believe in the pursuit of truth and humanity's ability to discover it. At Yeshiva University, Torah study is part of every day for every student. We can answer Rava confidently that we do make a lot of time for Torah study. In our general studies, we engage in the dialectics of wisdom. With our minds, we plumb the depths of knowledge in the pursuit of truth in every subject to help you become critical thinkers who are able to analyze, synthesize, and integrate your learning into your lives.

2. **Torat Adam** (Discover Your Potential): We believe in the infinite worth of every human being. It's reflected in the way we treat strangers and friends, professors and security guards, those we love and those we struggle to understand. It's the way Hashem created us. Our job is to find the *tzelem*, the Godliness, in everyone. At Yeshiva University, we believe in the importance of healthy relationships and the gift of family life and continuity. Every child is a bet on our future, a symbol of hope in tomorrow. This too is an expression of Torat Adam. It all begins with the dignity and respect we accord every single person.

3. **Torat Chaim** (Live Your Values): We believe in bringing our values to life. Yeshiva University prepares and expects its graduates to behave ethically in life and at work. We make sure, for instance, that all our business students study ethics, with the expectation that they will apply what they know of Jewish law to conduct themselves with the highest moral standards. We try hard to answer to a higher authority.

4. **Torat Chesed** (Act with Compassion): We believe in the responsibility to reach out to others with compassion. Be

kind, and kindness will shape you. Share your heart and your smile with others to alleviate their suffering. You will see examples of a Torat Chesed ethos everywhere and on every campus. You will see it in *chesed* opportunities, in the work of our Student Council, in club activities, and through the work of our extraordinary counseling services. You will feel it through the individualized care of our staff and faculty and through the work of our Office of Student Life. A life of meaning is a life of mercy.

5. **Torat Tzion** (Bring Redemption): We believe that humanity's purpose is to transform our world for the better and to move history forward. Hashem will not ask us, according to Rava, if we *waited* for redemption. He asks each of us if we *anticipated* it: *tzipita le-yeshua*. Anticipation is much stronger than simply waiting. A *tzofeh* in Tanach is a sentinel who is not just sitting back and waiting to see if something happens; rather, he is actively and vigilantly seeking out ways to help. We must play a participatory role in bringing about redemption.

I have seen and experienced these core values all throughout my life as my relationship with Yeshiva University began even before I was born.

My mother, Rosalie Bayer, was a graduate of Stern College. My father, Teddy (Tobias) Berman, was a graduate of Yeshiva College. In fact, they were each elected president of the student body of their respective schools and actually met at an event they planned together to celebrate Rabbi Samuel Belkin's (1911–1976) eighteenth year as Yeshiva University's president.

Throughout my childhood, it was a given that I would attend Yeshiva University's high school and college. I began my days as a student here in high school and studied in YU institutions or affiliated institutions throughout all of my formative years.

I mentioned this at my investiture speech as president, delivered in the historic Nathan Lamport Auditorium in 2017:

> I first stepped into this room when I was thirteen years old as a student of the Marsha Stern Talmudical Academy. Since that moment, I have been inspired and nourished by Yeshiva University. My studies – high school, college, graduate school, ordination, post-ordination, and my early teaching career – all occurred at YU. I even met my wife, Anita, when I was a senior in high school at an MTA-Central event. Intellectually, spiritually, and socially, I am a product of this special institution. Most new presidents of universities need to learn the story of their institutions to understand their narrative and their purpose, but I do not need to read a history book to understand Yeshiva University. It is in my heart, and it is in my soul.

Even my professional pursuits were intertwined with Yeshiva University. After my years in Yeshiva University's *kollelim*, studying under Rabbi Hershel Schachter and then Rabbi Aharon Kahn in the Kollel Elyon, I was selected to serve as a *Ram* (Teacher) in the Stone Beit Midrash Program. At the same time, I began my rabbinic career at one of the leading congregations that has a long and storied association with Yeshiva University – The Jewish Center of Manhattan. I served under my teacher, Rabbi Jacob J. Schacter, for six years, first as his intern, then as Assistant Rabbi, and finally as Associate Rabbi. When Rabbi Schacter moved to Boston, I became the synagogue's Senior Rabbi. I still maintained my classes at Yeshiva University, until the Yeshiva University administration decided that we could better maximize my time with the students if we formed a kollel that would travel to The Jewish Center. In that capacity, I became a *Rosh Kollel* for YU; a group of *semicha* students came to study daily with me at The Jewish Center, nourishing me and them and keeping me within the YU orbit.

Life was going well. My family integrated well into the Upper West Side community. I believed in my work, I loved my congregation, and I was teaching Torah on a very high level. Intellectually, spiritually, and professionally, my wife, my children, and I were settled and thriving.

At the same time, we were not in Israel.

We live in a generation in which Hashem has blessed us with the return of the Jewish people to our homeland. Israel is once again protected by a Jewish army under Jewish sovereignty. The hand of Hashem in history is obvious to all who have read through Tanach and have a sense of the trials and triumphs of the Jewish national journey. It was difficult for us to imagine that with this historic shift to Jewish autonomy in our own country, we would not try to raise our children in Israel and see how we could participate, in whatever small way, in the great Jewish project of our generation – building the Jewish state.

So Anita and I, with our then four children, took a sabbatical and informed the congregation that there was a very strong chance we would be staying in Israel.

And that's exactly what happened.

I left. I left Yeshiva University. I left our community and all that was deeply familiar. I began a new life. I studied and completed a doctorate in Jewish thought at Hebrew University and began a new career as a professor at Herzog College, sitting on its executive council and launching a new venture for them as director of Heichal Shlomo, the former home of Israel's Chief Rabbinate.

While the teachings and philosophy of Yeshiva University continued to nurture and enrich my life, and I stayed abreast of YU events over the years, it was more part of my past than my future.

Yet I sit here now at my desk in the president's office of Yeshiva University. What happened? Why am I here? The short answer is that I am here to write these letters to you. Like you, I am preparing for my final exam. But the longer story will unfold throughout the pages of this book. Rabbi Soloveitchik once said that successful educators open a window into their own souls. This story is in part uniquely my story. For some, the places and people who populate my story will be deeply familiar; for others with less familiarity with the YU community, the ideas and values will perhaps be more resonant. My hope is that all will find themselves in their journey. I will do my best to explain, and I invite you to write your own personal story and discover its uniqueness.

Thank you for joining me in this journey.

Warmest regards,
Ari Berman

Letter #3

A Time for Big Decisions

My Dear Student,

I applaud your decision to study at Yeshiva University. This decision will likely influence many other decisions that will make an imprint on your future, such as your choice of friends, your choice of major, your choice of profession, possibly your choice of spouse, and your choice of community. It all begins here.

I have personally faced these kinds of decisions all of my life.

Like many of you, one very consequential decision was where I would study post–high school. When I graduated, I left the small world I knew so well and began to feel more inspired and challenged by my Jewish tradition and teachings. That decision taught me that sometimes you have to leave home to find home.

Learning at Yeshivat Har Etzion was a major turning point in my life, as the gap-year experience is for many of you. Externally, I stopped wearing jeans and T-shirts and adopted the "uniform" of what I thought a *ben Torah* was supposed to wear: a polo shirt and Dockers. Looking back on it now, it's funny how we used these externalities to make statements about changes that were happening on the inside. Even during my years at YU, we used clothes to define us, sometimes without bothering to articulate and interrogate the values that lay behind our choices.

Clothing also created artificial divides during those years, like between those who dressed more casually and those who dressed in black and white every day. It was only afterward, when I moved into the world beyond YU, that I realized how small these differences were in the larger scheme of our most important commitments. The Torah brings us together in terms of our values and behaviors; these are the truly important things.

But beyond the superficial expressions of change, there were deeper, internal shifts taking place in my heart and mind. The sense of responsibility to study Torah that I had already felt for years previous was now coupled with a real enjoyment of learning. For the first time, I truly appreciated the depth of a *sugya* (a passage of Talmud) and its conceptualization. I understood there was a layered conversation taking place in the text and around it. I saw role models of *hatmada* (devotion to learning) all around me in the *beit midrash*, and I met rabbis who shaped my thinking and halachic observance.

Mori ve-Rabi Rabbi Aharon Lichtenstein *zt"l* was the first person to really open my eyes in terms of growth in learning. Due to his influence, I started to learn Torah seriously. My days in yeshiva were filled with pouring over Torah texts, hour after hour, in the *beit midrash*. It was there that my appreciation for Torah developed and my passion for learning was sparked. It was also Rabbi Lichtenstein who helped me understand and appreciate the *madda* in Torah U-Madda.

At times "not during night or day" (*Menachot* 99b), I started to explore many works of great literature. I was inspired by Rabbi Lichtenstein's breadth and depth in matters of Torah and in academic disciplines. The first book that I loved was Thomas Hardy's

Tess of the D'Urbervilles. There was deep poignancy in reading about Tess's pain and, on some level, I even suffered with her and took solace in the way she observed the world. Who could not be moved by Hardy's description of her: "She moved about in a mental cloud of many-coloured idealities, which eclipsed all sinister contingencies by its brightness"? I also began to read Russian literature in English translation. Leo Tolstoy and Fyodor Dostoevsky accompanied me during my years of study in Israel. So much of what they wrote spoke truth to my own experience of the human condition.

But even more than assisting my personal self-discovery, the great works of literature gave me entrée into experiences I never had. The complexity of the human experience that I saw in literature brought a new range of emotions to light for me. Many other people travel to expand their world; from my perhaps more narrow confines, reading was my grand exposure to humanity more broadly construed. Rather than taking away from my learning and religious growth, reading added to my spiritual pursuits, expanding my understanding of the human heart, its sorrow and its delights. Through story, I felt I was gaining a better understanding of the world and of myself.

I learned in Har Etzion for two years. During my second year there, my relationship with Rabbi Lichtenstein intensified. When I started at Har Etzion, I just hoped he would know my name. But by the time I left, I had a *rebbi*. I learned and grew during my years there, and that relationship with a *rebbi* who introduced me to a different way to study Torah and approach life colored the rest of my life.

After spending two years on a mountaintop in Israel studying Torah, I returned to New York to attend Yeshiva University with an intensified religious passion. There I discovered newfound challenges and developed close friendships that would guide me through the years there and continue to inspire me today.

But just like leaving home, only when I left YU did I really begin to understand YU. I'll explain what I mean in the pages ahead.

In the meantime, settle into your new environment. Enjoy dorm life, as I did. Take pleasure in your studies. Meet new people. Introduce yourself to our terrific faculty. Spend time in the library or in the *beis*. Get to know New York. Walk the paths of Central Park or the boards at Chelsea Pier. Peruse the shelves of the New York Public Library or the paintings at the Met. Relish late-night shwarma on the Wilf campus or sushi at Stern with friends. Maybe I'll see you at Chop-Chop or Tiberias.

These are the experiences that will turn into memories that will stay with you forever.

Warmly,
Ari Berman

Letter #4

The Call
That Changed It All

My Dear Student,

Every time we open a Tanach, we encounter a hero or heroine, prophet, judge, or king who stood before an important decision: a calling. Noach was called upon to build an ark. Avraham was called upon to build a nation. Moshe was called by Hashem to free a nation. Mordechai called upon Esther to protect a nation.

We look at these important heroes from the past as sources of inspiration and guidance for us. Your calling may not be as clear as a voice from *shamayim*, heaven, calling you to a life-changing task, but these stories remind us of the importance of seeing our purpose in some way as a call from Hashem to service. They tell us to reach higher and to see mission-driven work as a contribution to society. We are all destiny's children.

I've always seen my own life path as a mission and calling. It is why I chose the rabbinate. And I remember sitting in my office in Jerusalem at Heichal Shlomo when I literally received a call: Would I be interested in becoming the president of Yeshiva University? My initial reaction was "no." I had made *aliya*, lived in Gush Etzion, and was working in the heart of Jerusalem. My family had already made the challenging transition in our acclimation to life in Israel from the Upper West Side of Manhattan. It was difficult enough to uproot our family the first time. Why would I want to do that again?

Then I started to receive calls from the leadership at YU, including my *rabbeim*. They shared with me in greater detail the current needs and opportunities at YU. From them I began to sense that there was a historic moment to inspire a transformation. The needs at YU were not simply matters of financial prudence, but a fundamental reconsideration of our educational framework that could shape the future of Judaism in the Diaspora.

From my early conversations with mentors, rabbis, professors, and community leaders, it became increasingly clear to me how essential a strong Yeshiva University is to the greater Jewish project.

I remember one such conversation in which a world-renowned Jewish philosopher told me that the most important community in the Jewish world today is the Yeshiva University community. For at Yeshiva University, the students learn how to effectively embrace and balance the multitude of Torah values, enabling them to serve as living bridges to the different segments of the Jewish people and the world at large.

After that conversation, I took this possibility more seriously and spoke with my family about what this would mean for our lives. The most important relationships I have in life are with my wife and children, parents and siblings. I would consider this possibility only if it could work for our family, because a decision like this would, no doubt, shape the contours of each of our lives.

After much deliberation, we reached the point that we were ready to explore this further.

I found the search committee and YU's trustees to be genuine and sincere potential partners. They understood the importance of YU and wanted to see it rise to the prominent place of influence necessary to lead the Jewish world during these evolving times. One of the themes that consistently emerged from our conversations was the need to articulate the values of our community more clearly. Our communities across North America and around the globe are clearly connected. We are bound together, and there is a need to spell out the worldview that emanates from our yeshiva and that unites and inspires a large swath of the Jewish community throughout the world.

The need to articulate that worldview was underscored in my first few months as president. My family had not yet moved to America when my responsibilities began, so I stayed on campus in the Morgenstern Dormitory for three months. I suddenly found myself back in the YU dorms – but this time, I stayed in Rabbi Soloveitchik's former apartment. Of course, just being in Rabbi Soloveitchik's apartment was deeply intimidating. Every night, when I returned from very long days in meetings, I spent hours learning. It seemed like an affront to the Rav's memory to go to sleep!

Eventually, I found a productive rhythm. During those early months, I spent hours talking to YU students late into the night. One of the questions I consistently asked them was "What does YU stand for?" I could readily detect that our students struggled with answering this question. Some said, "Torah U-Madda." When I asked what that meant, I was often met with mixed explanations, ranging from the philosophical to the sociological. My own experience with the "brand" of Torah U-Madda, dating back to when I was a student, led me to understand intuitively that the term alone does not fully capture the philosophy and experience of Yeshiva University students and faculty.

What I found in my initial months was an incredibly mission-driven faculty, wonderful students, excitement and energy about learning…and also a strong desire for clarity about what we really stand for. Our motto was well known. It was on buildings and sweatshirts. Expanding on the motto as a way of life is more complicated.

It was then that I realized the real calling was more than taking on a job, even a really demanding one. The real calling is addressing the values proposition of an Orthodoxy engaged with the world. We need to bring to modern life a worldview that is saturated with Torah and filled with meaning. It's about trying to create a different educational conversation – one around values – that addresses the multi-faceted life of traditional Jews in dialogue with our surroundings and that uses our teachings to elevate those around us.

In order to begin this conversation with you in earnest, I want to introduce you to the giants who shaped Yeshiva University and made this conversation possible.

B'vracha,
Ari Berman

Letter #5

Standing on the Shoulders of Giants

My Dear Student,

When I entered Yeshiva University as an undergraduate majoring in philosophy, I knew that the beauty of learning Torah would not be compromised by my evolving appreciation of literature and philosophy. To tell you the truth, I didn't even really understand then what majoring in philosophy meant. I just wanted to spend time asking the big questions and learning how Aristotle, Descartes, and John Stuart Mill saw the world.

When it came to philosophy, I found myself asking Rabbi Michael Rosensweig everything – not just about Gemara, but also about major ideas in Western thought. I could ask him about a Ramban and Rambam and about Plato and Aristotle.

My schedule was demanding, to be sure, but it reflected a fresh commitment to developing my new interests. If I encountered tensions in the worlds I was navigating, there were also people to speak to about them. I didn't expect this path to be conflict-free. I faced contradictions and times when I had to filter the "secular world" rather than accept everything I read and saw wholesale. But I did regard *all* of my studies as part of Torah in the most expansive sense of that word. I understood the power and wisdom of the first *midrash* in *Bereshit Rabba* (1:1), which describes the way Hashem created the world using Torah as its blueprint:

בְּנֹהַג שֶׁבָּעוֹלָם מֶלֶךְ בָּשָׂר וָדָם בּוֹנֶה פָּלָטִין, אֵינוֹ בּוֹנֶה אוֹתָהּ מִדַּעַת עַצְמוֹ אֶלָּא מִדַּעַת אֻמָּן, וְהָאֻמָּן אֵינוֹ בּוֹנֶה אוֹתָהּ מִדַּעַת עַצְמוֹ אֶלָּא דִּפְתְּרָאוֹת וּפִנְקְסָאוֹת יֵשׁ לוֹ לָדַעַת הֵיאַךְ הוּא עוֹשֶׂה חֲדָרִים הֵיאַךְ הוּא עוֹשֶׂה פִּשְׁפְּשִׁין. כָּךְ הָיָה הַקָּדוֹשׁ בָּרוּךְ הוּא מַבִּיט בַּתּוֹרָה וּבוֹרֵא אֶת הָעוֹלָם. וְהַתּוֹרָה אָמְרָה בְּרֵאשִׁית בָּרָא אֱלֹהִים, וְאֵין רֵאשִׁית אֶלָּא תּוֹרָה, הֵיאַךְ מָה דְּאַתְּ אָמַר: ה' קָנָנִי רֵאשִׁית דַּרְכּוֹ.

In the way of the world, a king of flesh and blood who builds a castle does not do so based on his own knowledge, but rather based on the knowledge of an architect, and the architect does not build it based on his own knowledge, but rather has scrolls and books in order to know how to make rooms and doorways. Similarly, Hashem gazed into the Torah and created the world. The Torah states, "Through the *reishit* Hashem created [the heavens and the earth]," and *reishit* means Torah, as in the verse "Hashem made me [the Torah] the beginning [*reishit*] of His way" (*Mishlei* 8:22).

The Torah was Hashem's blueprint, the lens with which the universe was constructed. I realized and became more convinced that nature, thought, and experiences are all part of a life of religion and piety. My reading also supported this. Dostoevsky wrote in *The Brothers Karamazov*, "The awful thing is that beauty is mysterious as well as terrible. God and the devil are fighting there, and the battlefield is the heart of man." I felt that in only two sentences, he had beautifully captured our own battleground between the *yetzer ha-tov* and the *yetzer ha-ra*. There, Dostoevsky stated what Viktor Frankl would later regard as the basis for logotherapy in *Man's Search for Meaning*: "The mystery of human existence lies not in just staying alive, but in finding something to live for." I too had to search my heart to understand what I should live for and how to navigate the battlefield ahead.

I came to understand that my Torah learning and my curiosity to know more about the world inside and outside myself are the bricks that Hashem used as the Divine Architect who created the world with intention and purpose.

Over the years, I also took an interest in other architects, human builders – specifically those who founded Yeshiva University and built it into one of the leading faith-based universities. I appreciated what the founders set out to do and how the university evolved over its 135 years. As I said at my investiture as president, "When Yeshiva was founded in the early twentieth century, it met the needs of an Orthodox Jewish immigrant population with limited higher education possibilities. Over the generations, our specific form and structure has shifted depending on times, needs, and circumstances, but the core mission has always remained the same."

Rabbi Dr. Bernard (Dov) Revel (1885–1940) was one of YU's chief architects. He was the first president of Yeshiva from 1915–1940 and an Orthodox rabbi and scholar. Dr. Revel originally thought he would become a lawyer, but he earned a doctorate from Dropsie College instead and chose a different path. He was concerned that many young Jewish men would be lost to assimilation; they needed a place in which to study and train for vocations where their faith would remain intact and they would not face antisemitism in the pursuit of the American dream.

When Dr. Revel became president, he had a vision for Yeshiva that was both descriptive and aspirational:

Yeshiva aims at unity, at the creation of a synthesis between the Jewish conception of life, our spiritual and moral teaching and ideals, and the present-day humanities, the scientific conscience and spirit to help develop the complete harmonious Jewish personality, once again to enrich and bless our lives, to revitalize the true spirit and genius of historic Judaism.

To honor Dr. Revel, Yeshiva created the Bernard Revel Graduate School of Jewish Studies. He was a man whose genius was appreciated outside of Yeshiva as well. In 1986, four decades after his death, he even appeared on a $1 postage stamp as part of the Great Americans Series.

His is one of many names you'll see on both the uptown and downtown campuses. Some of the others are the names of generous philanthropists who believed in Bernard Revel's vision, and other names recall those who helped build the foundational structures – both the buildings and the ideas.

Rabbi Dr. Samuel Belkin, for example, was the second president of Yeshiva, from 1943 to 1975. His name graces many spaces at Yeshiva, and an award is given in his honor every year at the Benjamin N. Cardozo Law School. He was a Jewish scholar of note and an institution builder. Under his leadership, Yeshiva expanded and became a full-fledged university with multiple graduate schools of law, psychology, social work, and medicine. Dr. Belkin brought offerings in science and the humanities under the same roof as high-level Torah studies. These founders of Yeshiva University, Dr. Revel and Dr. Belkin, were known not only for their erudition in academic scholarship; they were also recognized as major *talmidei chachamim*, classical scholars of Jewish texts.

One of the crowning achievements during Dr. Belkin's tenure was the establishment of Stern College in 1954 with a major gift from Max Stern. Just two years after he awarded Eleanor Roosevelt with an honorary doctorate, he welcomed the first class of thirty-three female Jewish leaders on its campus at 253 Lexington Avenue. It provided these young women with a liberal arts education infused with Torah study in the heart of New York City. My aunt Dottie (Gewirtz) Berman was in Stern's second class. She graduated in 1959. My mother, Rosalie (Bayer) Berman, was in Stern's fifth class and graduated in 1962.

One outstanding student, Karen Bacon, graduated from Stern as the valedictorian of her class. She went on to earn her doctorate in microbiology at University of California and then came back to us in 1977 as the Dean of Stern College. In 2015, after decades of service, Dean Bacon was promoted to The Mordecai D. Katz and Dr. Monique C. Katz Dean of the Undergraduate Faculty of Arts and Sciences, serving as the undergraduate dean of both Stern and Yeshiva College. I rely on her competency, commitment, and intelligence to guide me and our undergraduate academic programs. She has given over fifty years of service to this institution and has been a personal role model for me of dedication.

Of course, one of the names you hear most frequently at Yeshiva is that of the Rav, Rabbi Joseph B. Soloveitchik (1903–1993). Born into an illustrious family of Lithuanian scholars, the Rav succeeded his father, Rabbi Moshe Soloveitchik, as the *Rosh Yeshiva* of RIETS, serving in that capacity from 1941–1986. His towering intellect and penetrating insights into the Talmud and about the life of faith made him the ultimate exemplar of our worldview. His philosophical works capture a rich religious experience fully shaped by the Halacha and reveal a righteous soul, one that could see in a sunset the onset of halachic time and find God's hand in the return of Jews to Israel through lines in *Shir Ha-Shirim*.

One of the Rav's most enduring contributions to Jewish thought is his reading of the two Genesis stories of human creation, which is developed most fully in *The Lonely Man of Faith*. According to the Rav, the two accounts in chapters 1 and 2 reflect two archetypes of human nature: Adam I and Adam II. Adam I is a creative being, stirred by ambition to steward, dominate, and build – as is reflective of Genesis 1, in which God commands him to multiply, to be fruitful, and to conquer the world. In this account of the story, the first couple was created at the same time, suggesting that the work ahead would be demanding and would require partnership.

Adam II emerges from chapter 2 of Genesis and reflects a very different side of human nature. This Adam was born alone, from a combination of earth and the breath of God. His job was not to work the Garden, but to watch it. Only later was Chava created from Adam's rib and brought to him after a lengthy search for companionship that included the entire animal kingdom. The Rav called Adam II a person of the spirit, who is less a builder and more a poet, artist, and philosopher. This Adam observes the world rather than seeking ways to improve it.

The Rav regarded these two Adams as present in every one of us. At times, we work in partnership; we experience friendship and feel a sense of belonging to a community. We learn to create and to contribute and change the world as we know it. At other times, we feel aware of our loneliness, our distinctiveness, and how unlike we are from every other human being. We observe and watch the world around us.

In his presentation of the richness, depth, and layers of each individual, the Rav speaks to the fact that Torah addresses all aspects of humanity: our drives, ambitions, hopes, and dreams. The Torah addresses our primal need for companionship and our preference, at times, for solitude. Our reverence for our past is coupled with our natural impulses to build a better future. The comfort of God's presence accompanies our human quest for excellence.

At Yeshiva University, we believe in cultivating these two aspects of humanity. Every day here, you should feel that both of these powerful instincts are addressed. Each student is invited to observe, to study, and to think, and also to explore, to soar, and to create. Spend time alone in contemplation and self-discovery. Enjoy the companionship of new friends with whom you can visit the sick, teach math in a local public school for underprivileged children, or travel to Europe on a humanitarian mission to help refugees. Volunteer in Washington Heights or in midtown Manhattan.

The Torah taught at Yeshiva University is rooted in the worldview of the Rav, recognizing and embracing the full multidimensional nature of each individual and contextualizing one's entire self in service to God.

I join you in the quest.

B'vracha,
Ari Berman

Letter #6

Torah U-Madda

My Dear Student,

Rabbi Dr. Norman Lamm (1927–2020) was the third president of Yeshiva University.

When he died, I was already installed as YU's fifth president. I opened my eulogy for him expressing the depth of my own sorrow at his passing: "We have lost a leader and a legend, a friend and a father." He was all of those things to me. He was a mentor and sage; an exemplar as a pulpit rabbi of a synagogue, The Jewish Center of Manhattan; and one of my greatest teachers in the art of life.

I began to develop a close relationship with Rabbi Lamm when I was twenty-four years old. Because I had read so many of his books and articles and heard him speak at YU so often, I felt that I already knew him on some level. But this was soon eclipsed when I actually spent personal time with him and realized how his writings, however magnificent, could never fully express the essence of his genius.

At twenty-four, I became a rabbinic intern at The Jewish Center, the congregation Rabbi Lamm regularly attended, and I asked him for feedback on my sermons. As a young rabbi, I was a novice in need of a guide, and I knew I would benefit immensely from his influence. Maybe it was chutzpa that drove me to ask for his time, but if Rabbi Lamm thought it was chutzpa on my part to ask, he never mentioned it. Quite the opposite. He spent time with me after every occasion I spoke in public, coaching me and inviting me to rethink the way I said something. He wanted me to hear the music of a sermon – not only its words, but its cadences as it was experienced by the audience.

During the time we spent together, we discussed much more than sermons. I listened carefully as he gave me professional and relationship advice, pearls of wisdom that inform who I am today.

It was Rabbi Lamm who took the words "Torah U-Madda," the motto of Yeshiva University, and offered its long conceptual history in his book entitled *Torah Umadda*. Its subtitle speaks to the disparity that can exist between these different spheres: *The Encounter of Religious Learning and Worldly Knowledge in the Jewish Tradition*.

Rabbi Lamm wrote the book at an inflection point for Yeshiva University. After experiencing a period of great expansion, YU was sending newly minted graduates into the world in careers as educators, rabbis, businesspeople, scientists, speech pathologists, lawyers, occupational therapists, and doctors. They were well prepared for lives as Torah-true Jews by virtue of their training and grounding in learning, prayer, and community building. They received all of this during their undergraduate years. Yet Rabbi Lamm saw that there was a need to articulate a guiding educational philosophy that would encompass different ways that Torah U-Madda has been understood. These ways sometimes complement each other and at other times clash. The approaches

Rabbi Lamm developed are associated with different scholars and disciplines.

In *Torah Umadda*, Rabbi Lamm writes in an autobiographical note that when he came to Yeshiva as an undergraduate in 1945, he was seeking a place where he could "continue his talmudic studies with a good college education under one roof." This was especially important because he was considering a career in the rabbinate. The idea of the melding of two worlds that each entranced him was central to his decision to come here and to his professional trajectory more generally. As he writes:

> I have experienced a lifelong romance with this ideal, a romance that was not at all uncritical. It has inspired and frustrated me, challenged and puzzled me, and made me feel that, in turn, it is incapable of theoretical justification for a believing Jew – yet so self-evident as not to require any justification.

Rabbi Lamm experienced these tensions, he writes, as a student, a faculty member of YU, and even as YU's president. As an undergraduate, he believed that a number of his fellow students felt the same way: "The big void in my education was the lack of a cohesive halakhic and philosophical theory of Torah Umadda." With the help of others, he began a series of programs and fellowships on several levels to help students understand the educational values that underpin Yeshiva University, and he began speaking about it himself.

The result was the book. There, he presented six justifications or models of Torah U-Madda understood and practiced differently by Jews of various religious commitments, but all valid and important. I will summarize them here briefly in my own words, without doing them justice. Rabbi Lamm used a colorful variety of Jewish texts and famous rabbinic figures to illustrate each approach. I encourage you to read the book and think about it as you form your own ideas about what it means to live a Torah-saturated life while benefiting from and contributing to the larger world in which we live.

> **Rationalist:** We engage in academic studies in order to understand and appreciate the world God created. It makes rational sense that since God created the world, it is our job to understand it. We cannot do that if we focus only on religiously edifying subjects but skip history, physics, or any other subject that explains our existence and our complexity.

> **Cultural:** Society offers us music, art, literature, museums, theater, and a variety of lenses that help us view our Jewish lives in relation to the norms of the world around us. We do so with appreciation but also with a filter. This integration can deepen our appreciation of human nature, while providing a powerful Jewish, halachic framework to interrogate the values of the surrounding culture. This approach is perhaps best summed up in another expression, popularized by the German rabbinic luminary Rabbi Samson Raphael Hirsch: "*Torah im derech eretz.*" Torah that endures has the capacity to influence the mores of society.

> **Mystical:** In this view, we study the world because nothing escapes God's notice. Everything is holy. If we believe, as the mystics did, that everything is truly sacred, then there is nothing off limits for our full intellectual and spiritual attention.

> **Instrumental:** Just as the mystical view is all expansive, the instrumental approach is limiting. We use academic studies

in order to better appreciate and understand the Torah. Mathematics is instrumental in understanding certain *sugyot* of the Talmud. Literature can help us better interpret biblical narrative, recognize its patterns, and develop its themes. Economics can assist us in thinking about the management of loans in the sabbatical year. And these are only a few examples.

Inclusionary: This approach envisions the world as a form of Torah. If the world is itself Torah, then it is our responsibility to study it. Studying the world is also an act of studying Torah.

Chasidic: In the Chasidic tradition, the ordinary becomes sanctified when it is framed by holiness. Thus, for example, food becomes holy when we make blessings before and after we eat it. Academic studies become holy when we learn them within a framework of sanctity.

In his conclusion, Rabbi Lamm wrote that there is "no model of Torah Umadda that is exclusively valid for all people at all times. There is a plurality of versions or paradigms to choose from." In other words, while certain sages or certain Jewish approaches have been associated with one group or another, advocates of Torah U-Madda may integrate these worlds in different ways in their own lives. A person can engage in academic studies instrumentally and then find these studies so deeply enriching that they become sanctified in his or her mind.

I was personally grateful that my own *rebbi*, Rabbi Aharon Lichtenstein, helped me initially in my thinking about what Yeshiva University stands for – the on-ramp, if you will, to my own articulation of the five Torah values. In his article "A Consideration of Synthesis from a Torah Point of View," Rabbi Lichtenstein frames the discussion within Moshe's clarion call to Hashem: הוֹדִעֵנִי נָא אֶת דְּרָכֶךָ, "Let me know Your ways" (*Shemot* 33:13). In studying the world, we study God's ways. Rabbi Lichtenstein shares the sensibility we should feel in trying to bring together two worlds that do not always meld organically:

> Few matters concern us – both disturb and affect us – more than the relationship between our religious and secular studies. As students committed to Torah and the study of Torah, and yet deeply engaged in the pursuit of a general education, we feel – and should feel – a strong need to understand the respective positions of the two areas of our lives.

In his thinking, when these values are in conflict, we should approach the confrontation using three fundamental principles:

1. Torah is always our primary and supreme value.
2. The achievement of a life of Torah is dependent on an ongoing commitment to Torah study.
3. We recognize the value of academic studies, not only as they contribute to the development of professional and vocational training, but also as a "general orientation toward the innumerable pragmatic exigencies of life."

Rabbi Lichtenstein believed that we need to know the world because sometimes we need to question what we see, hear, and learn: "We cannot combat worldliness until we know what it stands for; we cannot refute the secularist unless we have mastered his arguments." In this, Rabbi Lichtenstein was echoing a well-known teaching from *Pirkei Avot* (2:19): הֱוֵי שָׁקוּד לִלְמֹד תּוֹרָה וְדַע מַה שֶׁתָּשִׁיב לְאֶפִּיקוֹרוֹס, "Be diligent in the study of the Torah and know how to answer the heretic." We apply ourselves both to the study of our values and to what contradicts them, in order to protect ourselves. Rabbi Lichtenstein then raises our study of worldly disciplines beyond protection to actual influence: "If we wish not merely to react to our environment, but to act upon it, we must be thoroughly familiar with its mores and values."

Rabbi Lichtenstein saw great worth in the pursuit of knowledge. Many disciplines are "not only helpful but indispensable." He did not label such studies as Torah, following the approach of the mystics in Rabbi Lamm's schema, but "at the very least *heksher talmud Torah*," a means for understanding the Torah better. Such learning is formative to our spiritual development. In this respect, I am personally compelled by Rambam's well-known adage: וּשְׁמַע הָאֱמֶת מִמִּי שֶׁאֲמָרָהּ, "Accept the truth from whoever states it."

What I appreciated most about Rabbi Lichtenstein's perspective is that while he believed the Torah in combination with worldly knowledge, especially the humanities, could enlighten us about the complexity of human experience, at the same time, he was unafraid to ask difficult questions about synthesis. Even if academic studies are worthwhile, are they important enough to divert our attention from the *beit midrash*? In his words:

> [M]any have objected that, quite apart from the time which they consume, secular studies weaken the individual's religious position simply by diverting his interest, thus sapping his personal resources... Diversification leads both to diversion and distraction; it leaves the student involved with irrelevant matters but unmindful of his vital religious concerns...

This is a valid and important practical concern.

Rabbi Lichtenstein was also troubled by what he called "intellectual schizophrenia." Being pulled in multiple directions can damage the tender fibers of faith. "Ideas are potent. They are powerful agents, directly affecting the growth of our spiritual personality."

I kept these issues top of mind as a student, trying to live up to Rabbi Lichtenstein's chief standard for Yeshiva University students – commitment:

> Commitment is the permanent recognition, both emotional and intellectual, that Torah is our principal concern. Whatever else we may be doing, we know that Torah and its study, the conscious development of our spiritual personality, is the main thing. Compelling reasons may temporarily force us to lay it aside; but we can hardly wait to return.

Commitment is not only reflected in our behaviors. It is also a mindset, one that is reaffirmed when I put on *tefillin* each morning and recite these verses from *Hoshea* (2:21–22):

וְאֵרַשְׂתִּיךְ לִי לְעוֹלָם וְאֵרַשְׂתִּיךְ לִי בְּצֶדֶק וּבְמִשְׁפָּט וּבְחֶסֶד וּבְרַחֲמִים.
וְאֵרַשְׂתִּיךְ לִי בֶּאֱמוּנָה וְיָדַעַתְּ אֶת ה'.

And I will espouse you forever: I will espouse you with righteousness and justice, and with goodness and mercy, and I will espouse you with faithfulness; then you shall be devoted to the Lord.

We don't just do acts of piety and justice. We affirm our commitment to them daily. We commit to commitment, if you will.

Your studies at Yeshiva are, in the ideal, an education in commitment.

Torah is not a college major. It's *the* major.

Warmest regards,
Ari Berman

The Five Core Torah Values as Our Tree of Life

My Dear Student,

Until now, I have shared with you some of the wisdom of Yeshiva University's luminaries, who built this great institution on an educational ideology that includes the best of Torah and the best of academic studies. I believe firmly that an education at Yeshiva provides a framework for our generation for a life of meaning, purpose, and sanctity – one filled with *yirat Hashem* and *ahavat Hashem*, reverence and love for God.

But I also believe that although the motto of Torah U-Madda reflects the daily schedule of a Yeshiva University student, it is helpful to have additional language to describe the multilayered worldview and educational philosophy of our Torah community. In considering the entirety of the human experience and the larger question of what Hashem truly wants from us, we benefit from a more comprehensive and expansive use of language, which can move us toward answering central questions:

> How can all of the demands of modern life come together under a Torah framework?

> How should *chesed, tzedaka,* and social justice shape a Torah-true way of life?

> Where does Israel fit in as both a central and defining aspect of Jewish identity and as a practical homeland for our graduates?

> How does study, prayer, and connection to Hashem factor into our lives when the majority of our days post-university are spent on work and communal matters?

> What do we filter out from the "outside" world, and what do we allow into our homes and our hearts?

> How do we balance the multiple values that are required of us to truly live as *avdei Hashem,* God's servants?

In so many ways, in so many areas of our lives, the motto of Torah U-Madda is critical but insufficient to capture our spiritual complexities. While Torah U-Madda remains core to our definition, we are better served when we can understand the background values that inform this educational model. Passing Rava's test requires more than mastering Torah U-Madda.

Consequently, when I began my tenure as president, I initiated an effort to formulate our core Torah values so our students will better understand the Torah worldview that is expressed in every part of our students' day – both in our curricular and extracurricular activities, from the classroom to the dorm room, during the week and on Shabbat.

In my own thinking and deliberations about the matter, I found the language of my distinguished predecessor, President Richard Joel, very helpful. President Joel spoke often about how a Yeshiva University education both ennobles and enables. He promoted the way our Yeshiva brings wisdom to life, adding an eternal flame to the emblem of YU. His approach highlighted that the advantage of a Yeshiva University education is both intellectual *and* moral, combining a deep sense of history with a drive to bring our values out into the world with pride and enthusiasm.

The metaphor I picture in speaking about these values is a flourishing tree. Throughout our tradition, a Torah life is often described as a tree that thrives given the right conditions and nurturing. This powerful image is captured in the very first *mizmor* of *Tehillim* (*Tehillim* 1:1–3):

אַשְׁרֵי הָאִישׁ אֲשֶׁר לֹא הָלַךְ בַּעֲצַת רְשָׁעִים וּבְדֶרֶךְ חַטָּאִים לֹא עָמָד וּבְמוֹשַׁב לֵצִים לֹא יָשָׁב. כִּי אִם בְּתוֹרַת ה' חֶפְצוֹ וּבְתוֹרָתוֹ יֶהְגֶּה יוֹמָם וָלָיְלָה. וְהָיָה כְּעֵץ שָׁתוּל עַל פַּלְגֵי מָיִם אֲשֶׁר פִּרְיוֹ יִתֵּן בְּעִתּוֹ וְעָלֵהוּ לֹא יִבּוֹל וְכֹל אֲשֶׁר יַעֲשֶׂה יַצְלִיחַ.

Happy is the person who has not followed the counsel of the wicked, or taken the path of sinners, or joined the company of the insolent; rather, the teaching of the Lord is his delight, and he studies that teaching day and night. He is like a tree planted beside streams of water, which yields its fruit in season, whose foliage never fades, and whatever it produces thrives.

The life of Torah is described as a tree near abundant waters. In my understanding, the roots and basis for the growth of the tree is **"Torat Emet,"** truth. The blessing we recite every morning on the Torah thanks Hashem for giving us a Torat Emet and planting within us eternal life: אֲשֶׁר נָתַן לָנוּ תּוֹרַת אֱמֶת וְחַיֵּי עוֹלָם נָטַע בְּתוֹכֵנוּ.

When I use the term *emet*, "truth," I mean it with all of its implications: the God who is *emet*, our Torah that is *emet*, and our constant intellectual pursuit of *emet*. Our lives must be lived and modeled to seek *emet*. These are the roots that form and sustain each person throughout his or her life.

In the Torah, human beings are compared to a tree: כִּי הָאָדָם עֵץ הַשָּׂדֶה (*Devarim* 20:19). **Torat Adam** recognizes that each tree is different; no two trees are the same. Each is formed from the roots out of which it is nourished. This is essential to our educational philosophy of individualization. We do not believe in a religious model in which one size fits all. From the roots of the Torah, each individual develops, and each tree grows in its unique way.

The tree's branches represent how we bring our Torah to life, **Torat Chaim**. The Torah is *our* tree of life, as we read in *Mishlei* (3:18): עֵץ חַיִּים הִיא לַמַּחֲזִיקִים בָּהּ וְתֹמְכֶיהָ מְאֻשָּׁר, "It is a tree of life to those who grasp it, and those who draw near it are fortunate."

But what kind of life is reflected through our Torah? As the preceding verse indicates, we understand that a life filled with *mitzvot* and fulfilling God's will in the world is a life filled with **Torat Chesed**, loving-kindness: דְּרָכֶיהָ דַרְכֵי נֹעַם וְכָל נְתִיבֹתֶיהָ שָׁלוֹם, "All its ways are pleasant, and all its paths brings peace" (*Mishlei* 3:17).

The goal and outcome of a life filled with Torah and *chesed* as its branches is to bring redemption to the world. This is the fruit, flowers, and foliage that never fade but are always regenerating.

וְהָיָה כְּעֵץ שָׁתוּל עַל פַּלְגֵי מָיִם אֲשֶׁר פִּרְיוֹ יִתֵּן בְּעִתּוֹ וְעָלֵהוּ לֹא יִבּוֹל וְכֹל אֲשֶׁר יַעֲשֶׂה יַצְלִיחַ.

He is like a tree planted beside streams of water, which yields its fruit in season, whose foliage never fades, and whatever it produces thrives. (*Tehillim* 1:3)

We believe that the beginnings of redemption's blossoming can be seen in the return of Jewish sovereignty in our homeland. We are stalwart and firm Zionists, for whom supporting the State of Israel is an essential principle. And we also believe that Israel itself is a vehicle through which to bring greater redemption to our entire society: חַדֵּשׁ יָמֵינוּ כְּקֶדֶם, "Renew our days as of old" (*Eicha* 5:21).

This is **Torat Tzion**.

That is what Hashem is asking us to do with this one amazing life we have, with our tree of life – to nourish and to be nourished, to grow and to help others grow, to bring our gifts out into the world with kindness, and to use all of this to advance and improve the world.

The image of a tree provides a framework from which to understand our values, both individually and collectively. No one core value exists without the other. Each is interconnected and balanced by the others. In the letters ahead, we will discuss and unpack each one of these core values in greater detail.

Sometimes, if you're lucky, you will meet a person who embodies all five of these qualities, a living *etz chaim*. One of these Torah giants and one of my prime role models is Rabbi Hershel Schachter. In addition to studying his Torah in our kollel when I was studying to be a rabbi, I have learned from him by watching his example, especially in my own time of vulnerability. When my uncle passed away from Covid on the eve of Passover, the burial restrictions created significant halachic challenges, and I called Rabbi Schachter to receive his guidance. It was such a raw and painful time for me because, at the time, I was my uncle's prime caretaker. At that moment, I needed counsel from one of the greatest living halachic minds. After my conversation with him, I spoke with Rebbetzin Schachter. She shared with me that her husband was crying throughout the conversation.

Rabbi Schachter exquisitely combines Torat Chaim with Torat Chesed. His approach to Halacha and to each individual is filled with deep love and caring. Indeed, he personifies all of our core Torah values. His dedication to Torat Emet, his complete commitment to his students' personal development in their Torat Adam, and, of course, his profound love for Israel are matchless. When I was rabbi of The Jewish Center, I asked Rabbi Schachter to speak to our shul for Yom Ha'atzmaut because I wanted my congregation to see a rabbi steeped in Torah who loves Tzion so much you can feel it when he speaks.

My blessing to each of you, our dear students, is that you find such a role model, and learn how to live lives of great meaning and purpose. Start with the truth of the Torah that is disseminated from generation to generation. Value yourselves and find value in every individual. Bring your values to life with kindness and help move our communities toward justice for all.

Be the tree. Grow sturdy roots. Touch the sky.

B'vracha,
Ari Berman

Seeking Truth: Torat Emet

My Dear Student,

I would like to take each of these five core Torah values and explain to you why each one is so central to the ethos of Yeshiva University.

We begin where we should begin – with the truth, Torat Emet. We believe that over three thousand years ago, Hashem gave the Torah to Moshe at Mount Sinai. We believe that in that Torah there are eternal values that are not subject to the vagaries and vicissitudes of time. It is this pursuit of truth that animates our intense study of Torah at all hours, which, in turn, deepens our relationship with God. It is that truth that catalyzes our desire for all knowledge.

Please understand that this belief in truth is deeply countercultural in our current intellectual climate. We live in a time in which truth is under assault. We live in an age of fake news where basic facts and assumptions about the universe are questioned or attacked. So much of higher education today promotes relativism, subjective narratives, and competing versions of the truth. It's not that anyone is attacking the Torah per se. Something more insidious is taking place, and something more nuanced is being questioned: People don't believe that there is any truth to be sought.

This worldview undermines not only religious studies, but also academic studies.

In my early years as president, I attended a conference for presidents of universities, and in a small session, the presidents were discussing a question that is regularly asked in today's academy. Should academic freedom be limited to the extent that a professor cannot call for acts of violence against those with competing views? Sadly, this was not a purely theoretical question; it describes the lived reality on the ground. At the end of the conversation, I pointed out to the group that the focus of the conversation was on "negative freedom," the limits of what the university should tolerate. But I queried my peers about the other side of the coin, "positive freedom."

What is the purpose of the university today? Historically, the university is designed as an institution in which students and faculty seek and pursue the truth. All great research is driven by this overarching purpose. The canon of Western literature developed organically over time, focusing on the books and works of art that most genuinely and perceptively depict the state of the world and the human condition. But what happens to a university that can no longer judge a book on its own merits? In one session at the conference, the former president of Harvard offered a presentation, and I was so struck by the incongruity of the current and past perceptions of the purpose of the university that raised a question about the slogan on Harvard's crest. Can a university today subscribe to "veritas" if it fundamentally challenges the very notion of truth?

In his book *Thinking, Fast and Slow*, Daniel Kahneman demonstrates how vulnerable we are to the popularity of opinions: "We know that people can maintain an unshakable faith in any proposition, however absurd, when they are sustained by a community of like-minded believers." How we develop beliefs about truth and falsehoods is, of course, a much larger discussion for a different time, but it highlights the gap between the current intellectual milieu and our long-standing Torah perspective. We must weigh and judge social trends carefully and not be pulled into every current.

It is our pursuit of truth that animates our intense study of Torah during the day and deep, deep into the night. As the Zohar teaches, קֻדְשָׁא בְּרִיךְ הוּא תּוֹרָה אִיקְרֵי, "The Holy One, blessed be He, is called the Torah." The Torah and God are one. By studying the truth of Torah, we better understand the truth of God.

One of my *rabbeim* once explained this concept to me by describing the experience of reading a great work of literature. After reading Tolstoy, one cannot tell how Tolstoy looked or dressed or went about his day. But one better understands Tolstoy by knowing his concerns, values, and goals. Similarly, by studying Torah, we don't learn what Hashem "looks like," but we better understand and draw closer to God by engaging with and studying these divine ideas and concepts.

This pursuit of truth is the reason that the primary *derech ha-limmud* (method of study) in our yeshiva is *iyun*, in-depth study. Based on the methods of Rabbi Soloveitchik, who was both an heir to and an innovator of the great Brisker tradition, the large majority of the *shiurim* of our yeshiva primarily follow in that rigorous and analytical path, as we are seeking to uncover, categorize, and analyze the ideas and principles of our tradition. For Rabbi Soloveitchik, the ideal "Halakhic Man" internalizes this deep understanding of the talmudic tradition, so that Halacha becomes the prism through which one experiences life and the basis on which a true Jewish philosophy is formed. This critical, analytical approach informs all our Torah studies, including our study of Tanach, Halacha, and Jewish thought.

Over the years, we have incorporated additional approaches into our tracks of study, including more courses on Jewish thought, *mussar*, and *Chassidut*. We have informal *chaburot* and *va'adim* for all of our undergraduate programs, which are group study opportunities to discuss how to operationalize what we study and be accountable to our learning. We have also created more academic courses in Jewish studies as the interests of the student body have widened. All of this is in pursuit of penetrating the truths found in the Torah. As Rambam writes in *Hilchot Yesodei Ha-Torah* (Laws of the Foundations of the Torah 2:2), a greater grasp of the majesty and wonders of the world is the path to greater awe and love for God.

It is for this reason that it is very important that you, our students, challenge yourselves and push yourselves in your course selection and classwork. With our dual curriculum of both Torah and college courses, we expect you to be ambitious and productive in all of your educational pursuits. In a success-driven culture, it is common for one to take the course with an easier route to a better grade, but we encourage you to take courses that will stimulate you and leave you with a better understanding of humanity, the world, and society. Taking classes for an easy A is not cheating, but it is cheating yourself of a world-class education. Challenge yourself. When you coast and put in little effort you deny yourself the beautiful immersion in learning and the gift of being truly present in the moment. Not showing up to class is wasting the valuable tuition dollars that are being invested in your education.

You have only a few years of your lives in which the vast majority of your time is devoted to this kind of intellectual exploration. Get the most out of these years by putting yourself in situations that open new vistas, allowing you to experience new horizons in your pursuit of knowledge. This is a once-in-a-lifetime opportunity to meet professors, be inspired by our rabbis and Jewish educators, stretch yourself, and question.

Take advantage of the time now. Believe me, you will greatly appreciate it later.

B'vracha,
Ari Berman

Letter #9

A Life of Honesty and Integrity

Dear Student,

In our tradition, the centrality of truth, *emet*, is not just about study. Truth is also a moral mindset. We strive to live lives of deep integrity. This too is rooted in our relationship with God. Integrity in our tradition is not only a strategy for success, but a principal way in which we draw closer to God by emulating God's ways. Repeatedly, we are taught in our primary texts that ה' אֱלֹהֵיכֶם אֱמֶת – our God is a God of truth.

The Talmud teaches that חוֹתָמוֹ שֶׁל הַקָּדוֹשׁ בָּרוּךְ הוּא אֱמֶת, Hashem's very seal is truth (*Yoma* 69b). A seal is like a signature; it is a unique object that signifies an identity. When Moshe sought forgiveness on behalf of our people, he described Hashem as "truth" (*Shemot* 34:5–6). The psalmist writes about Hashem, צִדְקָתְךָ צֶדֶק לְעוֹלָם וְתוֹרָתְךָ אֱמֶת, "Your righteousness is eternal, and Your teaching is true" (*Tehillim* 119:142). And every day, twice a day, we conclude the *Shema* by proclaiming that Hashem is *emet*. God is Truth.

Moreover, God judges unfavorably those who lie, because they enhance falsehood and diminish the Divine in our world (*Sota* 42a). We are told explicitly in the Torah that truth should be our calling card: וְלֹא תְכַחֲשׁוּ וְלֹא תְשַׁקְּרוּ אִישׁ בַּעֲמִיתוֹ, "You shall not deal deceitfully or falsely with one another" (*Vayikra* 19:11). We are directed not only to preserve truth, but also to distance ourselves from lying, cheating, and deceiving, as the verse teaches, מִדְּבַר שֶׁקֶר תִּרְחָק, "Keep very far from dishonesty" (*Shemot* 23:7).

This is why I feel deeply humiliated if I hear about students cheating at YU. I feel similarly if there is some report of an observant Jew who is found to have committed a white-collar crime. These are serious breaches of Jewish law. But for some reason, in some parts of our community, these kinds of activities are not viewed as transgressions. Somehow, one can still consider oneself a *ben* or *bat Torah* even if he or she cheats on a quiz, a lab report, or a final exam. This never works if you want to ace Rava's final exam though. How does this not challenge the religious identity and self-perception of those who engage in this egregious, unethical, and unacceptable behavior?

Perhaps they convince themselves that it's not so bad since no one is being harmed, even though the person they are deceiving is their instructor and the ones they are harming are their fellow students. But they are also harming themselves. They become the kind of people who carry within themselves the shame and danger of deception, which augurs poorly for their futures. Research has confirmed that those who cheat in one area of life are liable to cheat in another.

But it can be difficult to make the right choice.

If the path of truth were easy, the Torah would not have to demand it so many times and in so many ways. The very first human beings struggled with deception. Adam hid from an all-knowing God, Adam blamed Chava for giving him the fruit of knowledge, and Chava blamed the snake. No one acted with accountability in this story. This strain of deception is passed on to the next generation, when Kayin crafts a clever denial for killing his brother. God in both of these stories used questions as a mode of confrontation, trying to help each newly created being negotiate the difficulty of admitting errors. We lie to hide the shame of our mistakes. We tell the truth so that we do not get pulled backward due to past poor judgments we made.

I am always inspired when I witness people in business settings who clearly set a red line that they will not cross when it comes to their integrity. In these settings, I think of chapter 6 of *Mishlei*, in which we find a beautiful image of keeping true to one's convictions that starts with honoring the Torah your parents taught you and holding it tightly as a reminder of who you are:

נְצֹר בְּנִי מִצְוַת אָבִיךָ וְאַל תִּטֹּשׁ תּוֹרַת אִמֶּךָ.
קָשְׁרֵם עַל לִבְּךָ תָמִיד עָנְדֵם עַל גַּרְגְּרֹתֶךָ.
בְּהִתְהַלֶּכְךָ תַּנְחֶה אֹתָךְ בְּשָׁכְבְּךָ תִּשְׁמֹר עָלֶיךָ
וַהֲקִיצוֹתָ הִיא תְשִׂיחֶךָ.
כִּי נֵר מִצְוָה וְתוֹרָה אוֹר וְדֶרֶךְ חַיִּים תּוֹכְחוֹת מוּסָר.

Keep, my child, your father's commandment;
do not forsake your mother's teaching.
Tie them over your heart always;
bind them around your throat.
When you walk it will lead you;
when you lie down it will watch over you;
and when you are awake it will talk with you.
For the commandment is a lamp, the teaching is a light…
(*Mishlei* 6:20–23)

The consistency of tying תּוֹרַת אִמֶּךָ, your mother's teachings, to your heart is tested throughout our lifetimes. There are times in life that are legitimately confusing, in which a short-term dip on the other side of honesty might feel warranted for a long-term gain.

Once, early on in my career, I had an interview for a rabbinic position in which the board expected me to toe a particular line that was halakhically uncomfortable for me. Many counseled me to be circumspect in my position. I thought the opposite – namely, that it was important to lay out my thinking clearly and honestly, so the congregation and I would be able to assess accurately whether this position was right for me or not.

I turned to my teacher, Rabbi Lichtenstein, for his advice about what to do in this situation, presenting him with points I wanted to emphasize in the upcoming interview. I will never forget his response. "Ari," he said, "you will never get the job, but at least they will know what a *ben Torah* stands for."

When I did get the job offer, much to everyone's surprise, Rabbi Lichtenstein called and left a message to let me know how proud he was of me. I saved that message for the longest time. It taught me the importance of looking in the mirror and making an honest decision based on my own moral conscience in challenging situations, even when there is a lot at stake for me personally. Is this a decision about which my parents and teachers would be proud? Is this how Hashem would want me to act? Placing these questions in that framework is important not only because it clarifies the answers, but because it provides the inner strength to make difficult decisions that at times run against the grain. If you have the confidence that Hashem is by your side, every other consequence becomes minimal in comparison.

Our mandate in this world is to live a life of honesty, integrity, and appreciation for all that we have been given. At Yeshiva, we aspire to inspire every one of our graduates to seek truth and be committed to the Torah as our source of infinite and timeless wisdom.

This is not only the pathway to success, but also the path of the righteous.

Warmly,
Ari Berman

Letter #10

You Have Infinite Worth: Torat Adam

My Dear Student,

As we move from truth to humanity – from *emet* to *adam* – in our value system, we are moving from the roots to the tree, from the foundational, axiomatic posture that nourishes us to the living, animated creation that is supported by those roots: the self.

College is one of the most formative times in shaping the self. This is precisely what we want you to do at Yeshiva University. We want you to see this as *your* time, because our story of creation begins with the belief in *your* infinite worth. This is confirmed in a Mishna that likens Hashem's work to that of a craftsman (*Sanhedrin* 4:5):

שֶׁאָדָם טוֹבֵעַ כַּמָּה מַטְבְּעוֹת בְּחוֹתָם אֶחָד וְכֻלָּן דּוֹמִין זֶה לָזֶה, וּמֶלֶךְ
מַלְכֵי הַמְּלָכִים הַקָּדוֹשׁ בָּרוּךְ הוּא טָבַע כָּל אָדָם בְּחוֹתָמוֹ שֶׁל אָדָם

הָרִאשׁוֹן וְאֵין אֶחָד מֵהֶן דּוֹמֶה לַחֲבֵרוֹ. לְפִיכָךְ כָּל אֶחָד וְאֶחָד חַיָּב
לוֹמַר, בִּשְׁבִילִי נִבְרָא הָעוֹלָם.

When a person stamps several coins with one seal, they are all similar to one another. But the supreme King of kings, the Holy One, blessed be He, stamped all people with the seal of Adam, the first human, [as all of them are his offspring,] yet not one of them is similar to another. Therefore, [since all humanity descends from one person,] each and every person is obligated to say: "The world was created for me."

Hashem has one mold, yet every one of us has a different genetic makeup. The fact that we can be part of a species while retaining our individuality is extraordinary.

Like this Mishna instructs, we want you to say, "The world was created for me" while you are at Yeshiva. Because you are one of God's precious creations, ask yourself, "What am I here to do?" This is your time to discover your purpose and your gifts. This is not selfish. This is your world to build. You are here to do the important and sometimes difficult work of figuring out who you are, what you want to learn, what you want to do in the future, what you should look for in friends and a spouse, and where you want to live. No one will know you better than you know yourself. Others will help you on this journey of self-knowledge, but only you can truly develop your identity. This means not always striving to fit in. It means not being afraid to stand out, to buck convention, or to break out of the mold. Trying to be like everyone else, especially religiously, is damaging to the precious *neshama* that is yours alone. This can lead to endless unhappiness. Even when you leave the safe confines of YU, select your career path, choose a spouse and a community, you may be tempted to go with the crowd, and let the crowd make decisions for you. That would be a mistake. No one else can live your life, and you cannot live someone else's.

One of our *Roshei Yeshiva* and a cherished personal mentor, Rabbi Mayer Twersky, shared with me the thought that in our yeshiva, we do not believe in a prefabricated, one-size-fits-all notion of Judaism. It's all too easy when you're developing yourself in a community to look at what others are saying and doing and to pattern yourself on what you perceive is the norm. But these are only markers of possibility for you. You will have to listen, learn, and craft your own path. You are not here to imitate someone else. You are not a photocopy.

I remember well Rabbi Lichtenstein addressing two arenas of Halacha – what is *chova*, obligatory, and what is *reshut*, permissible – as models of self-construction. In Jewish law, as in Jewish life, there are obligations and there are choices. The Talmud describes that there were Sages who chose certain *mitzvot* in which they "specialized" and with which they were associated. Each of us should also have special *mitzvot* and areas on which we focus our learning, and favorite *tefillot* (prayers) that resonate with us more than others. These are hallmarks of the individual stamp and imprint we place on our Jewish lives. This imprint – this signature coin, in the words of the *Midrash* – is ours to fashion. It is our *reshut*.

But here, as in all arenas of life, balance is necessary. Too much focus on the self can generate narcissism and an inability to see and respond to the needs of others.

I don't have to tell you that we live in a society focused on the individual. In our day, algorithms confirm and amplify our personal tastes and customize the method and content of the news we hear, the music we listen to, and how we shop. We have so many choices – too many choices – that focus on our very specific needs and desires. This emphasis on the self has also led to societal problems of self-absorption, boredom, and loneliness, what Robert Putnam referred to as "bowling alone." Technology has been both a blessing and a curse in this regard. It has hyperconnected us, but it has also kept us overly attached to screens.

Rabbi Lord Jonathan Sacks, in whose memory we dedicated Yeshiva University's Rabbi Lord Jonathan Sacks-Herenstein Center for Values and Leadership, wrote often about the difficulty that all of these individual choices have caused. In *The Dignity of Difference: How to Avoid the Clash of Civilizations*, he writes:

> Never before have we been faced with more choices, but never before have the great society-shaping institutions offered less guidance on why we should choose this way rather than that. The great metaphors of our time – the supermarket, cable and satellite television and the Internet – put before us a seemingly endless range of options, each offering the great deal, the best buy, the highest specification, the lowest price. But consumption is a poor candidate for salvation.

I did not grow up in the age of cellphones and the internet. The music I listened to was whatever my peer group listened to and what the music industry offered us. We all got our news from the same few sources. But times have changed. I am conscious of the distractions and the noise that these new developments in technology have created and the intense focus on the self they promote.

To this challenge, our tradition offers a twofold response. In the words of the great Sage Hillel (*Avot* 1:14):

אִם אֵין אֲנִי לִי, מִי לִי, וּכְשֶׁאֲנִי לְעַצְמִי, מָה אֲנִי.

> If I am not for myself, who will be for me? And if I am only for myself, what am I?

The first half of Hillel's statement highlights that our tradition values the individual. But there is a difference between society's notion of equal rights for each individual, which emerges from a sense of fairness, and our tradition's deep-seated belief that every individual is holy. Individual *kedusha* is rooted in the notion of *tzelem Elokim*; each individual is created in God's image, and one's task in life is to nurture, actualize, and develop this holiness, the spark, and the soul that was given to him or her.

The movie *Chariots of Fire*, which was released in 1981, was based on the life of Eric Liddell, a Scottish runner who won gold medals in the 1924 Paris Olympics and tragically died in a Japanese internment camp in China before the conclusion of World War II. Liddell was born into a family of missionaries. In one scene in the movie, Eric's sister, who was always critical of him, confronts him and asks him why he is wasting his life running when he, too, could take his place in the family as a servant of faith. Liddell was, in fact, a deep believer, but he tells his sister that he will return to his missionary work in China only after he competes in the Olympics. In the movie, these are the words he used to explain himself: "I believe God made me for a purpose. He also made me fast, and when I run, I feel His pleasure."

We each experience God's pleasure and presence differently. God takes pleasure in our individuality. Our goal at YU is to help you develop *your* way. For us, education is not just a window into the world; it is a light into the soul. What you study helps develop your whole personality. Maybe you too are a runner, or an artist, educator, or healer. We are here to help you develop all aspects of yourself – to find the coin that is the currency of your life.

We hope that this spirit of individuality will be reflected in your time here and permeate everything you do. At YU, you will have ample opportunities to customize your education, to learn in small classes with individualized attention, and to get academic advisement and career counseling that is tailored to you. If you care to and make the effort, you will get to know our professors well and learn from them throughout your years here. They are role models of academic excellence. Ask them about their research interests as you form your own. If you need additional help in a subject, don't hesitate to ask. They are there for your intellectual growth. Make use of their office hours and develop relationships with them. This will enable them to know you well enough to advise you and write your letters of recommendation when it's time for your next chapter.

And we have a vast array of Torah opportunities for you on campus – more than any other yeshiva or college in the world – that are specifically tailored for each student. Every student can choose a customized path of Torah study, ranging from the foundations and fundamentals in our JSS/Mechina program for those without a strong Jewish studies background to the advanced Talmud, Tanach, and Halacha *shiurim* on both of our campuses.

You have powerful Jewish role models on campus in our rabbis and Jewish educators, as well as the students in our Jewish professional graduate programs. They have chosen to deepen their Jewish learning and commitment, some to pursue careers in Jewish service and others for the simple pleasure they take in learning.

Sanctifying the self is the essence of Torat Adam, the infinite worth and distinctiveness of every human being. This is a foundational pillar of who we are.

Internalizing this belief naturally leads to the second half of Hillel's statement and the second part of our response to the challenge that is posed by modernity's excessive notion of the self: If I am only for myself, what am I?

Because we believe in the dignity of every life, we must treat everyone with dignity. Just as you are created in the image of God, so is your roommate, the woman working the register at the cafeteria, and your political science professor. We believe in human majesty, and we value the individual and creative talents that enable us to partner with God. That means we believe that someone else has this same majesty, and it is our job to discover it.

It sounds obvious, but it is not always obvious in reality. Every single person on our campus must be treated with this kind of respect. This is what it means to create a sanctified community. It brings me joy when I see our students walk over to a YU employee with a friendly hello or when a new student who feels lonely is met with a kind, embracing smile. We are here to create community, each of us, as holy coins stamped with God's presence and our own uniqueness.

Once you value yourself, you are better positioned to value others.

This capacity for responsiveness to others is what we call Torat Chesed, a core value we will discuss in greater depth later.

Your college years are a time to build your character, to figure yourself out, and to stand before big life decisions. It's also a time of great possibility and important questions:

Who am I?

Who do I want to be?

Where am I in my religious journey?

These questions echo what we learn in *Pirkei Avot*, Ethics of the Fathers: "Know from where you came, to where you are going, and before whom you are destined to give an account and a reckoning" (3:1).

As you embark on this voyage, keep in mind the words of Rabbi Soloveitchik about the importance of staying true to yourself and not trying to imitate others:

> I may have very few good traits, but one trait which I do possess is my inability to imitate anyone else. I always want to be myself and to display my unique dignity of having been created in the image of God. The glory of the individual is

exemplified by the singularity of every human being. This concept is the motto of my life.

The Rav believed that this emphasis on individuality is the essence of a Yeshiva University education and a way that Yeshiva is distinctive. When the Rav came to America, people advised him to fit in with societal norms. He refused precisely because he understood that if he did that, he would be compromising on his own unique and infinite worth:

> I knew that I would lose my originality if I tried to be what I was not. I would lose my uniqueness, and ultimately the Divine Image within me. I do not like to do what others can do better or just as well. I wish to do that which I am unique at! This is not an expression of haughtiness; no, it is a fulfillment of my intrinsic human dignity and individuality.

We are here to help you fulfill your intrinsic human dignity and find your path. The questions you are asking now about yourself and your future are perfectly normal and part of the Torat Adam journey. Our faculty, *rabbeim, mashgichim,* and Jewish educators are here to talk to you. They care about your future, and they will make time for you. Academic Advising and the Shevet Glaubach Center for Career Strategy and Professional Development are part of the support network of Torat Adam that we provide. We take pride in the hard work of our Office of Student Life. Our remarkable YU Counseling Center is here for you when you *want* to talk and when you *need* to talk. If you are in pain, know that your pain is our pain. You are not alone. Please know that we are here for you.

The Rav understood that Yeshiva can assist students in their pursuit of Torat Adam, as he wrote, "This school is unique, and it is imbued with the honor and dignity of man created in the Image of God. This is the secret of my love for and commitment to the

Yeshiva." If I could speak to the Rav today, I would tell him that it is no secret. Here at Yeshiva University, we are committed to facilitating your unique development.

Best wishes in your travels,
Ari Berman

Letter #11

Tefilla: Prayer as an Expression of Torat Adam

My Dear Student,

In my eyes, *tefilla* (prayer) is one of the ultimate manifestations of Torat Adam. This might seem counterintuitive at first. It would be natural to regard *tefilla* as an act of community, because we are directed to pray in a *minyan, tefilla be-tzibbur*. But in our tradition, as articulated by Rabbi Soloveitchik, *tefilla* is a very personal expression of our service to Hashem.

Although *tefilla* allows an entire congregation to access Hashem's holiness together – as we often cite the verse בְּרָב עָם הַדְרַת מֶלֶךְ, "A numerous people is the glory of a king" (*Mishlei* 14:28) – it is fundamentally a service of the heart, as interpreted in the Gemara in *Ta'anit* (2a):

"וּלְעָבְדוֹ בְּכֹל לְבַבְכֶם": אֵיזוֹ הִיא עֲבוֹדָה שֶׁהִיא בַּלֵּב, הֱוֵי אוֹמֵר:
זוֹ תְּפִלָּה.

"You are to serve Him with all of your heart": What can be
described as service of the heart? Prayer.

In the thought of the Rav, this service of the heart emerges from
the depths of one's soul. Rabbi Soloveitchik begins his work *The
Lonely Man of Faith* with a confession:

> I am lonely. Let me emphasize, however, that by stating "I
> am lonely" I do not intend to convey to you the impression
> that I am alone. I, thank God, do enjoy the love and friend-
> ship of many. I meet people, talk, preach, argue, reason; I
> am surrounded by comrades and acquaintances. And yet,
> companionship and friendship do not alleviate the pas-
> sional experience of loneliness which trails me constantly.
> I am lonely because at times I feel rejected and thrust away
> by everybody, not excluding my most intimate friends, and
> the words of the Psalmist, "My father and my mother have
> forsaken me," ring quite often in my ears like the plaintive
> cooing of the turtledove. It is a strange, alas, absurd experi-
> ence engendering sharp, enervating pain as well as a stimu-
> lating, cathartic feeling. I despair because I am lonely and,
> hence, feel frustrated. On the other hand, I also feel invig-
> orated because this very experience of loneliness presses
> everything in me into the service of God.

For the Rav, the person who is lonely is never actually alone. The
Rav writes poignantly in a number of places about how throughout
his life – even in the darkest of times, such as when he was being
wheeled into surgery or when he was heartbroken in grief over the
passing of his wife – Hashem accompanied him and comforted
him. This sentiment is aptly captured in the Rav's use of Plotinus,
the Neoplatonic philosopher of late antiquity, to describe prayer
as the act of "a lonely and solitary individual" reaching out to a

God in "His transcendental loneliness and numinous solitude." Prayer is the flight of the alone to the alone. The one who is alone reaches out to the One who can only be alone. We are, each of us, profoundly alone at times, and it is in those times that we reach out to the God who is similarly singular in presence. It is this feeling of being completely and intimately alone that creates a deep connection to Hashem, as we open ourselves in vulnerability, and that lies at the heart of *tefilla*.

This perspective on prayer helps mediate the well-known debate regarding whether the obligation to pray daily is from the Torah or is of rabbinic origin. Rambam maintains that the obligation to pray daily is from the Torah, as he writes in *Hilchot Tefilla* (Laws of Prayer 1:1), as well as in the fifth *mitzva* of the *Sefer Ha-Mitzvot*:

מִצְוַת עֲשֵׂה לְהִתְפַּלֵּל בְּכָל יוֹם שֶׁנֶּאֱמַר "וַעֲבַדְתֶּם אֵת ה' אֱלֹהֵיכֶם". מִפִּי הַשְּׁמוּעָה לָמְדוּ שֶׁעֲבוֹדָה זוֹ הִיא תְפִלָּה שֶׁנֶּאֱמַר "וּלְעָבְדוֹ בְּכָל לְבַבְכֶם" אָמְרוּ חֲכָמִים אֵי זוֹ הִיא עֲבוֹדָה שֶׁבַּלֵּב זוֹ תְפִלָּה. וְאֵין מִנְיַן הַתְּפִלּוֹת מִן הַתּוֹרָה. וְאֵין מִשְׁנֶה הַתְּפִלָּה הַזֹּאת מִן הַתּוֹרָה. וְאֵין לַתְּפִלָּה זְמַן קָבוּעַ מִן הַתּוֹרָה.

> It is a positive commandment to pray each day, as the verse states, "And you shall serve Hashem, your God." The Sages learned that this service is prayer, as the verse states, "And to serve Him with all your heart" (*Devarim* 11:13), on which the Sages commented, "What may be described as service of the heart? Prayer." The number of prayers is not prescribed in the Torah, and the form of prayer is not prescribed in the Torah, nor does the Torah prescribe a fixed time for prayer.

In contrast to Rambam, Ramban (Nahmanides), in his gloss to the *Sefer Ha-Mitzvot*, regards prayer as mandatory from the Torah only in a time of crisis. As a proof text, he cites a verse about crisis:

וְכִי תָבֹאוּ מִלְחָמָה בְּאַרְצְכֶם עַל הַצַּר הַצֹּרֵר אֶתְכֶם וַהֲרֵעֹתֶם בַּחֲצֹצְרֹת
וְנִזְכַּרְתֶּם לִפְנֵי ה׳ אֱלֹקֵיכֶם וְנוֹשַׁעְתֶּם מֵאֹיְבֵיכֶם.

When you go to war against an enemy that attacks you in your land, you shall sound a *terua* (short blasts) on the trumpets. You will then be recalled before the Lord your God and will be delivered from your enemies. (*Bemidbar* 10:9)

When we were threatened in the wilderness, we prayed as a community in desperate straits.

The Rav explained the debate between these two scholarly luminaries by suggesting that fundamentally, they both agree that *tefilla* emerges from crisis; they differ only as to how to define crisis. While Ramban refers to "surface crisis," like during times of war and famine, Rambam speaks of "depth crisis," which emerges in the sensitive soul in everyday life. Every day brings its handful of challenges and questions. All of this – the joy and the despair – we bring with us when we *daven*. Every day, we have the opportunity to bring our whole selves into communication with Hashem.

The Rav eloquently describes this human need to pray:

> Prayer is a mode of expression or objectification of our inner experience, of a state of mind, of a subjective religious act, of the adventurous and bold attempt of self-transcendence on the part of the human being, and of his incessant drive toward the infinite and eternal.

The Rav writes elsewhere that "prayer is the tale of an aching and yearning heart." Torat Adam asks that we discover our true selves and bring those true selves into conversation with Hashem.

This approach to *tefilla* raises a very obvious question. Prayer in this respect makes the most sense if experienced in solitude. We know this from our own experiences as well. Sometimes – many times – we pray with the best *kavana* (intention) when we are by ourselves. Yet, the very language of *tefilla* always moves us from the individual to the plural. Our requests are made in the plural, and on Yom Kippur we even confess our sins in the plural. If *tefilla* is *avoda shebalev*, a service of the heart, why is it so communally focused?

The answer is that our tradition directs us to expand what is in our hearts. We must include others, both those close to us who may need our *tefillot* and, moving outward, strangers on the other side of the globe who are in crisis. The act of prayer is expansive. The heart has many chambers.

This notion emerged most poignantly for me personally when I was a congregational rabbi. I had very close relationships with many of my congregants. I felt their suffering when they were going through difficult times, and I was elated when they experienced celebrations. This transformed my whole *tefilla* experience. When we gathered together in prayer, I knew intimately the joys, struggles, and problems of people in every single pew – the woman in the front who was recently diagnosed with cancer, the young man who just got engaged, and the new father who just lost his job. There were so many people to hold in my thoughts. And I wanted to hold them there. These were my friends. They were my family. I loved them. My heart expanded, and, as a result, the service of my heart expanded as well.

This led to some practical challenges. As a congregational rabbi, I had to tend to the public *tefilla*, which impacted on my personal one. Even the amount of time I could spend on my private *Amida* (silent prayer) was curtailed due to my concern of burdening the congregation, as they would, out of respect, wait for me to finish my silent *Amida* before starting the public recitation. For a number of *tefillot* during the *Yamim Nora'im* (High Holidays), I instructed the congregation not to wait for me, so that I could devote myself fully to unburdening what I was carrying in my heart.

And it took time. I remember that one congregant came over to me during the break on Yom Kippur and quipped that he was a little troubled. "I thought we had a pretty pious rabbi, but there must be a mountain of transgressions you are repenting for!" If he only knew that my *tefilla* was actually about him and his current challenges, about his family, his neighbors, and his fellow congregants.

The Gemara (*Bava Kama* 92a) teaches us that כָּל הַמְבַקֵּשׁ רַחֲמִים עַל חֲבֵירוֹ וְהוּא צָרִיךְ לְאוֹתוֹ דָּבָר, הוּא נַעֲנֶה תְּחִילָּה – one who prays for another's needs, even if they are similar to one's own, is actually answered even more immediately.

When it comes to the true meaning of *avoda shebalev*, I have learned that it doesn't only mean *what's* in your heart. It's also *who's* in your heart. Who is in *your* heart, my precious student?

This kind of prayer redefines the notion of self. Channeling the words of the Rav in his explanation of the debate between Rambam and Ramban, if we profoundly feel the needs of others when we pray, then their crises become our own. When you love others enough, you absorb their pain, the way you absorb your own. Their joy also becomes your happiness. This is our aspiration for prayer.

The Gemara (*Shabbat* 10b) illustrates different ways that the *Amora'im*, the talmudic Sages, would prepare for prayer:

"הִכּוֹן לִקְרַאת אֱלֹהֶיךָ יִשְׂרָאֵל". רָבָא בַּר רַב הוּנָא רָמֵי פּוּזְמְקֵי וּמְצַלֵּי, אָמַר: "הִכּוֹן לִקְרַאת" וְגוֹ'. רָבָא שָׁדֵי גְּלִימֵיהּ וּפָכַר יְדֵיהּ וּמְצַלֵּי. אָמַר: "כְּעַבְדָּא קַמֵּיהּ מָרֵיהּ". אָמַר רַב אָשֵׁי: חֲזֵינָא לֵיהּ לְרַב כָּהֲנָא כִּי אִיכָּא צַעֲרָא בְּעָלְמָא, שָׁדֵי גְּלִימֵיהּ וּפָכַר יְדֵיהּ וּמְצַלֵּי. אָמַר: "כְּעַבְדָּא קַמֵּי מָרֵיהּ". כִּי אִיכָּא שְׁלָמָא לָבֵישׁ וּמִתְכַּסֵּי וּמִתְעַטֵּף וּמְצַלֵּי. אָמַר: "הִכּוֹן לִקְרַאת אֱלֹהֶיךָ יִשְׂרָאֵל."

"Prepare to greet your God, Israel" (*Amos* 4:12). Rava bar Rav Huna would don expensive socks and pray, and he said he would do this because it is written: "Prepare to greet your God, Israel." Rava would not do so; rather, in his prayer he would remove his cloak and clasp his hands and pray as a slave before his master. Rav Ashi said: I saw that Rav Kahana, when there was suffering in the world, would remove his cloak and clasp his hands and pray, as a slave before his master. When there was peace in the world, he would dress, and cover himself, and wrap himself in a significant garment, and pray, and he said that he did so in fulfillment of the verse "Prepare to greet your God, Israel."

The first two Sages prepared for *tefilla* based on their understanding of how best to approach Hashem in terms of what posture looked most respectful. But Rav Kahana prepared by first looking at his surroundings, internalizing the needs of those around him, and then collectively bringing everyone with him when he approached Hashem.

Torat Adam charges us to develop all our unique skills, talents, and qualities. But this is not simply for the purpose of self-actualization. It is to have a broader notion of self that includes others. This is the kind of Torat Adam that leads to a Torat Chaim that is also *ahavat chesed*; it leads to loving acts of loving-kindness.

It is the kind of Torah we teach in our yeshiva and the Torah to which I will now turn.

B'vracha,
Ari Berman

Torat Chaim: An Integrated Life and an Ancient Dilemma

My Dear Student,

Now we must take truth, *emet,* and the personal development of *adam* and ground it in life, *chaim.*

    The discussion about how best to live as a committed Jew did not begin at Yeshiva University. It is very ancient. One of the Talmud's most famous debates is about how to prioritize one's time for study with everything else that must get done (*Berachot* 35b). The Sages discussed the verse from the *Shema* that mentions the human role in agriculture: וְאָסַפְתָּ דְגָנֶךָ וְתִירֹשְׁךָ וְיִצְהָרֶךָ, "And you shall gather your grain, your wine, and your oil" (*Devarim* 11:14). This is hard work, work that must be done in order to support ourselves and our families. Yet we read in the first chapter in *Sefer Yehoshua* לֹא יָמוּשׁ סֵפֶר הַתּוֹרָה הַזֶּה מִפִּיךָ וְהָגִיתָ בּוֹ יוֹמָם וָלַיְלָה (1:8), "This Torah shall not depart from your mouths, and you shall contemplate in it day and night." Is it possible to farm, the Talmud ponders, if we are supposed to contemplate Torah both day and night, as Yehoshua mentions?

Rabbi Yishmael was of one opinion: Set aside time not only for Torah, but also for work. But Rabbi Shimon bar Yochai disagreed vehemently. He asked a reasonable question that was both rhetorical and also practical: "Is it possible that a person plows in the plowing season, sows in the sowing season, harvests in the harvest season, threshes in the threshing season, winnows in the windy season, and is constantly busy? Then what will become of Torah?"

This talmudic discussion concludes not with a ruling, but with a retrospective look at reality: הַרְבֵּה עָשׂוּ כְּרַבִּי יִשְׁמָעֵאל, וְעָלְתָה בְּיָדָן; כְּרַבִּי שִׁמְעוֹן בֶּן יוֹחַי, וְלֹא עָלְתָה בְּיָדָן – "Many have acted in accordance with the opinion of Rabbi Yishmael and were successful, and many have acted in accordance with the opinion of Rabbi Shimon bar Yochai and were not successful." There were people who followed both paths, but only one path was appropriate for the majority of people.

This conclusion highlights the importance of both paths, that of both Rabbi Yishmael *and* of Rabbi Shimon bar Yochai. For while the path of Rabbi Yishmael works for the majority of people, the subtle implication of the Gemara is that the path of Rabbi Shimon bar Yochai does work for a minority of people. And, in truth, we need that minority.

We need our rabbis, educators, Jewish intellectuals, thought leaders, *poskim*, and *talmidei chachamim* and *chachamot*. We need a segment of our population to fully and comprehensively focus on Torah studies, on learning, on teaching, and on preaching. And *Baruch Hashem*, at Yeshiva University we have RIETS, one of the most successful rabbinic schools in Jewish history, in addition to Azrieli, our graduate school of Jewish education. We have GPATS, a program for intense Torah studies for women and a center for

Torah thought and leadership, and we have the Bernard Revel Graduate School for Jewish academic scholarship. Collectively, the students in these institutions make up the intellectual, spiritual, and educational leadership of tomorrow for our community and beyond.

This is a critical path for our community in order to grow and develop. But it is not the only path, nor is it the path for the majority of our community. Consequently, we have other tracks that enable students to commit to Torah study while developing their skills and aptitudes in different directions, to become the next generation's computer scientists, social workers, philosophers, doctors, entrepreneurs, health professionals, accountants, and art historians, to name just a few examples.

The blessing of Yeshiva University is that we educate the wide expanse of the Jewish future – not just the *klei kodesh*, but the lay *kodesh*, as my predecessor, President Richard Joel, used to say. And we do so by embracing the whole student.

Still, the challenge laid out by Rabbi Shimon bar Yochai must be addressed. If you spend your whole day planting, harvesting, and winnowing, what will happen to your Torah?

It is this question that Yeshiva University's educational philosophy directly addresses.

I would like to unpack our approach through the role model of our patriarch Yitzchak. In *Bereshit* we read, וַיֵּצֵא יִצְחָק לָשׂוּחַ בַּשָּׂדֶה, "Yitzchak went out *lasuach* in the field" (24:63). What does the word לָשׂוּחַ, *lasuach,* mean? Rashi, quoting *Chazal*, teaches that *lasuach* means that Yitzchak was "praying" in the field. In fact, *Chazal* teach us that this verse is the source for *tefillat Mincha*, the afternoon prayer (*Berachot* 26b). However, Rabbi Shmuel ben Meir (Rashbam), Rashi's grandson, teaches that the literal reading of the word *lasuach* is "to plant." Yitzchak went out into the field to plant because, as we know from other verses, Yitzchak was a farmer.

To my mind, it is very telling that the same word *lasuach* can mean both planting and praying. For in this word lies a dual message: One must stop one's planting in order to *daven*, and one should view planting itself as an act of prayer.

It is very important for anyone in the workforce to heed Rabbi Shimon bar Yochai's warning not to get so caught up in work that one is too distracted to pray. We always need to find time in our day and workweek for *tefilla* and for Torah. It is no coincidence that the *tefilla* that Yitzchak initiated was *tefillat Mincha*, because it is the prayer that most highlights this point. We are almost always in the middle of something in the afternoon when we are called upon to pause and acknowledge Hashem in our lives.

The second part of the dual message of *lasuach* is that one's planting must be understood as a form of *tefilla*. Yitzchak teaches us that when you are out in the world and living by the Torah, even when you're planting, you're praying. That is also Torah.

There is beauty in describing both what Yitzchak literally did and what it signified with the same word. Our tradition does not want us to think of our lives as bifurcated, but rather as unified by Torah. This is Torat Chaim. What would it look like if every time we prayed, we planted something metaphorically, and if every time we planted something, we saw it as an act of prayer?

Rabbi Yitzchak Hutner (*Pachad Yitzchak, Iggrot U-Michtavim*, letter 94) was once asked for advice by a student who felt he was living a dual life, one at home in the religious world and one at work in a secular society. He could not live with the dichotomy. Rabbi Hutner answered that someone who has two houses with two wives and two families is living a double life, while one who has multiple rooms in the same house is not leading a double life, but a unified life with multiple facets. The point that Rabbi Hutner was making is that one must contextualize one's entire life as *avodat Hashem*, heavenly service in all of its aspects. One's whole life should be viewed in the context of Torah, so that it should appear unified and whole.

A similar story happened to me. Once in my travels, I met a father who shared with me that his son was troubled. His son used to study most of the day at YU, devoting much time to his *tefilla* and Torah learning, but upon graduation, he secured a much sought-after position in a high-profile business firm. Now he spends his days at work. His *tefilla be-tzibbur* is in a much faster-paced *minyan* than he was accustomed to at Yeshiva, and his time to learn each day is much more circumscribed. Where, his son wondered, is my *avodat Hashem*?

I answered the father that I was deeply moved by the question. Certainly we believe that his son's *avodat Hashem* is in his *davening* and learning, and he still needs to find the time to devote to that, but in our Yeshiva, I said, we teach that his *avodat Hashem* is also in his hours working in the business firm!

Both the content of his work done to increase human flourishing and the way in which he works with *mentschlichkeit*, honesty, and compassion are expressions of his *avodat Hashem*. In his current position, he has an opportunity to do a world of good. The way he models his Torah values, the way he interacts with all of his coworkers, colleagues, and people on the staff – all of this provides him with an opportunity to sanctify Hashem's name in the world.

The Talmud teaches (*Yoma* 86a) that the command to love Hashem is also a command to make the name of Hashem more beloved in the world: "וְאָהַבְתָּ אֵת ה' אֱלֹהֶיךָ", שֶׁיְּהֵא שֵׁם שָׁמַיִם מִתְאַהֵב עַל יָדְךָ. Every minute of this young man's day in his firm is an opportunity to show his love for Hashem.

This is the Torah we teach at Yeshiva University. This is what we stand for.

We stand for a Torat Chaim, a Torah that embraces life in all of its potentialities and sees every minute of every day as an opportunity to actualize our Torah and serve our Creator. This is perhaps best expressed by a verse in *Tehillim* (119:97) in which we once again find the verb *lasuach*: מָה אָהַבְתִּי תוֹרָתֶךָ כָּל הַיּוֹם הִיא

שִׂיחָתִי, "O how I love Your Torah! It is my occupation all day long." When you live an integrated life and when what you study informs who you are and what you do, then you are serving Hashem all day long, in everything you do.

In the *Shema*, we are mandated to walk with our faith. It surrounds us when we lie down and when we wake up. There is something kinesthetic about Torah. A life of Torah is not just sitting, studying, and *davening*. It is active and engaging. It is the way we breathe and move in the world.

This is why Torat Chaim comes after Torat Emet as part of our educational philosophy. Truth has to meet life. These values can live side-by-side or be in conflict with one another. We read in *Tehillim* (85:11), for example, that, חֶסֶד וֶאֱמֶת נִפְגָּשׁוּ צֶדֶק וְשָׁלוֹם נָשָׁקוּ, "Mercy and truth meet; righteousness and peace have kissed each other." This is an interesting image. Black-and-white truths that we might derive from reason, learning, reading, and thinking may soften to grey as these truths encounter reality. Truth can be rigid and unbending, but it must negotiate with real people in real-world situations. The values of seeking truth and making peace conflict at times, because we are human, inconsistent, and flawed, and because two people may see the world in very different ways. This verse reminds us that in an ideal world, truth and peace find a way to live together on intimate, close terms. Without Torat Chaim, Torat Emet can be flat and one-dimensional.

In Judaism, it has never been one or the other. There is a well-known question raised by the medieval sages as to why one says the blessing on studying Torah, לַעֲסֹק בְּדִבְרֵי תוֹרָה, only once a day in the morning, even though there are breaks in our day between the times one actually studies Torah, when one goes to work, tends to one's family, or takes care of communal matters. In other cases of blessings on *mitzvot*, such a gap of time would warrant the recitation of another blessing before performing the *mitzva* again. Tosafot famously answer that when it comes to learning Torah, there is no real break. Rabbi Soloveitchik explained this approach as rooted in the subconscious. Those who study Torah are like a mother who thinks about her children throughout her day when they are not with her, even when fulfilling other obligations and responsibilities. Similarly, the words of Torah are always with us throughout the day, even when one is not actively engaged in studying Torah. There is no break. Torah is always on one's mind.

Mori ve-Rabi Rabbi Michael Rosensweig adds a different nuance to answer this question. He argues that if one's actions and standards of behavior are based on one's learning, then living a life of Torah is also a fulfillment of the *beracha* לַעֲסֹק בְּדִבְרֵי תוֹרָה. Even when one is not actually studying, one is still considered "engaged" in Torah.

There is a *midrash* that praises Chanoch, a mysterious character from the earliest chapters of *Bereshit*. The *midrash* calls him a *tzaddik*, a righteous man. What made him righteous? The *midrash* explains that Chanoch was a cobbler, and with each turn of the needle, he declared, בָּרוּךְ שֵׁם כְּבוֹד מַלְכוּתוֹ לְעוֹלָם וָעֶד, "Blessed be the name of His glorious kingdom forever." Even repairing a pair of shoes can become sacred when we take pride in the work and dedicate it to God. In the frame of Rabbi Yitzchak Hutner that we saw earlier, Chanoch did not even have two rooms in his house. He had one expansive room in his soul that included all the parts of who he was.

For us at YU, the Torah is not only lived throughout the day through prayer and study; it is also in the front of our minds as a conscious lens when making decisions. Our behavior and character are all informed by Torah. The Rav once said that if he could write a fourteenth *Ani Ma'amin*, if he could add one principle to these iconic declarations of faith, it would be that the Torah applies in every generation, in every time, and in every place. It belongs in our classrooms and boardrooms, on the court and in a court, in our dining rooms and our dorm rooms, in the office and on vacation. We are not afraid that the Torah will lose its relevance. We don't need to hide it or be ashamed of it. We trust in its enduring value, its wisdom, and its relevance to any situation in which we find ourselves. It is what helps us pass Rava's test.

This approach to life enables us to see every moment of the day as holy and precious. It is hard to be well adjusted and happy when we think that the way that we spend the majority of hours is simply instrumental, a task to get through in order to support what we really want to do. We don't focus on the joy of work, and we risk dissipating the holiness of the work itself, no matter what job we have. We see what we do as separate from who we are.

But for us, work is also a *tefilla*, both in the content of what we are doing to support human flourishing and in the way we do it. This means working with integrity in finance, compassion in medicine, impartiality in law, and *menschlichkeit* in everything. Our *avodat Hashem* is expressed in the way we relate to our bosses, supervise employees, and treat customers. Every moment we are in the workforce, we have an opportunity to be *makadesh shem Shamayim be-rabbim*, to sanctify God's name publicly. We bring our values into the world and celebrate them.

This approach underlies a philosophy that I once heard explained by my teacher, Rabbi Jacob J. Schacter. One of the opinions in the *Midrash* is that the letter that marked Kayin's head after he killed his brother Hevel was a letter ו. Why would Kayin need to walk around his whole life with a ו? Because a ו in a sentence is a connector, the *"vav ha-chibbur."* It brings two parts together and says they can live in relationship to one another. Kayin's sin was that he split apart from others, and he needed to learn the importance of connection.

Building on this idea, my colleague Rabbi Moshe Tzvi Weinberg called this the philosophy of AND. In psychology, we call this dialectical thinking. Too often, we find people framing their choices in life as either/or. Kayin thought either he would succeed as beloved to Hashem or Hevel would be the beloved one. It was an either/or perspective. But the truth is in the "AND." It's not one or the other. It is both.

So many students are stuck in an either/or perspective. Instead, bring your full self, all of your spiritual *kochot* (strengths) and abilities, into your life decisions to determine where you can most excel and make a significant impact. When you discover that, you will have found your *avodat Hashem*.

This is an essential life lesson that naturally flows from our model of education, which focuses on the AND, the Torah AND the Madda.

This, at times, creates some tension for our students who begin YU immediately after they leave the intensity of a year or two in Israel, where they spent early mornings *davening* and late nights learning, with no tests and no grades, enjoying the gift of simply studying Torah full time.

A few years ago, I was speaking to some students in our post-Pesach program. They had just returned from Israel, and I asked them how they were finding YU. One of the students said that he was enjoying being here, but he found one element particularly difficult. In his past yeshiva, he said, if he missed *Shacharit* in the morning, one of his rabbis called to check up on him. At YU, he could miss *minyanim* and no one would know.

I explained to him that when he gets older and moves to a community to start the next phase of his life, no one will call him if he misses *minyan*. In that sense, YU is helping him transition to the rest of his life in the loving context of a yeshiva with *rabbeim* and educators who care. We are educating you to want to live an integrated life with personal responsibility, to be out in the world as a full *eved Hashem*, utilizing your entire range of *kochot* in the service of the Jewish people and all of society.

YU is your bridge to the rest of your life. It's the first time you have to be truly conscious of how you will balance many competing values and how you will integrate your Torah into your professional choices, your social choices, your dating, your volunteering, and your decision about the community in which you want to settle down. At this very impressionable time in your life, you will make decisions that impact the entirety of your life. These decisions will be even wiser if they are made in a spirit of wholeness and happiness.

Know that this is where Torat Chaim comes in. Some of our life goals will not involve the immediacy of holiness we experience when we recite a *mizmor* of *Tehillim* or learn in the *beit midrash* deep into the night. Keep in mind that there is immediate holiness and there is long-term holiness. Raising a family, for example, is central to living a Torah life. It is the best and most literal expression of Jewish continuity. There is little more meaningful in life than learning with one's children and passing down our *mesora* to the next generation. But as anyone who has children knows, along with all the gratifying hours are all the difficult physical and emotional demands. Similarly, going to work enables us to support our lives and contribute to society, but not every moment will be easy and fulfilling. One of our goals at Yeshiva is to help you experience the immediacy of *kedusha* and create a personal life-strategy that allows for the long-term pursuit of *kedusha*.

It should also be noted that there are challenges in living and working in a broader society that espouses values and mores that run counter to our Torah teachings. All parents know how difficult it is to help their children navigate the tension between tradition and an increasingly complex world. And this is also essential to our education. Located at the nexus between tradition and innovation, YU provides you with the tools for critical self-reflection. This can help you weather the storms and tempests of contemporary moral discourse, so that you leave here both rooted and nimble, anchored in our values and equipped with the language and sophistication necessary for success in the world in the years that follow.

We are uniquely qualified to raise engaged Jewish citizens, for whom Judaism is vibrant and essential to their lives and for whom work is vibrant and essential to their lives. Some of you come to campus with a full day-school education; some of you come from public school, with little to no previous Jewish education. Here at Yeshiva, you will find friends for life, and often soulmates and partners for life. Here at Yeshiva, you have the opportunity not only to *learn about* Judaism but also to *experience* Judaism, to appreciate that Shabbat is not just something we *keep*, it is something we *treasure*, and that living a life of faith adds significance and happiness to our lives.

Our yeshiva is fully committed to Torat Chaim. We are proud to offer a comprehensive, integrated educational program designed to produce the Jewish leaders of the next generation and beyond, who are firmly committed, forward-focused, engaged in the world, and pillars of society.

Your education here will transform your life, as it has already transformed the Jewish people throughout the world.

B'vracha,
Ari Berman

Be Kind: Compassion and Torat Chesed

My Dear Student,

Many years ago, when I was a rabbi at The Jewish Center, I needed to travel to Englewood, New Jersey, to pay a *shiva* call to a member whose father had passed away. I was living in Manhattan, and my wife had the car that day. I was discussing my logistical problem with my father, who lived in Queens. Immediately, my father volunteered a solution. He drove from Queens to my apartment – an hour away – then drove me another forty-five minutes to the *shiva* call, and then waited until I was finished to drive me back to the city.

This sort of kindness, of being present in whatever way he could be helpful, stands in my mind as a metaphor for what my father has always done for me throughout my life. Transported me. Supported me. Driven me to achieve more and to be a better person. From when I was a child until my adult years, his advice, support, and love have been essential to my personal development.

I attribute my sense of self to my mother's love. From the time I was very little, my mother expressed through words and actions how much she believed in me. I remember that when I was a child and all the adults were busy talking at the Shabbat table, if she thought I had something to say, she quieted everyone down to make room for my voice. She made me feel that whatever I had to say was important. And it made me feel like I was important.

No one is born into a *beit midrash*. We grow into Torah. Our first experiences in life are not about achievements. They are about being loved simply because our parents love us. Study, learning, and achieving are acquired disciplines and dispositions, activities in which we engage as we age and mature. But unconditional love is the first thing we experience.

This is similar to the love that God has for all of us, as was poignantly expressed by Yirmeyahu when he likened the people of Israel to a dear son and delightful child for whom God always has compassion (*Yirmeyahu* 31:19). בָּנִים אַתֶּם לַה׳ אֱלֹקֵיכֶם, "You are children to Hashem your God," Moshe says in *Devarim* (14:1), and *Chazal* point out that חִבָּה יְתֵרָה נוֹדַעַת לָהֶם – there is an additional element of love because Hashem makes known to us our special relationship with Him (*Avot* 3:14).

For me, Torat Chesed is bound up with this love. We come into a world swathed in love, a love that should spill over to others. Love is the key and driving force behind all *chesed*. As Rambam writes (*Hilchot Avel* 14:1–2) when codifying acts of kindness such as visiting the sick, comforting the mourner, and celebrating with a bride and groom, all of these rabbinically mandated acts of kindness are fulfillments of the Torah directive of וְאָהַבְתָּ לְרֵעֲךָ כָּמוֹךָ, "Love your friend as yourself" (*Vayikra* 19:18). Despite all of the difficulties entailed in loving another as we love ourselves, we have exemplars in the love of our parents, our friends, our spouses, and our God. By channeling that feeling and translating it into actions, we fulfill this positive commandment that stands at the center of our tradition.

In Tanach, one of the ways in which friends are referred to is with the Hebrew root מכ״ר, from the word for recognition. In *Totality and Infinity*, Emmanuel Levinas observes that our most intimate experiences emerge just from recognizing someone else's face: "The face is a source from which all meaning exists." It is this that helps us see God in the presence of another person: "In the face the Other expresses his eminence, the dimension of height and divinity from which he descends."

Every moment and every way we treat, act toward, and recognize others is a religious experience and one potentially filled with great meaning. This idea perhaps finds its greatest expression in the *Kodesh Ha-Kodashim*, the Holy of Holies chamber in the *Beit Ha-Mikdash*. The Ark of the Covenant is placed in the Holy of Holies, and on its cover are two *keruvim*, two cherubs who face each other. The spot in which the divine presence is understood to rest is right between these *keruvim*. The message is that God is found in between the gaze of two faces looking at one another.

At Yeshiva University, kindness is not simply an aspiration, as it is on most college campuses. Here it is an essential component of our educational philosophy. We express it in many ways, including many of the extracurricular activities organized through our Student Council and the Office of Student Life – such as food drives, visits to homeless shelters, and volunteer opportunities to teach science in local public schools. But at YU, *chesed* is not an extracurricular activity. It is an inherent and integral way we relate to each other.

There are so many opportunities here to express and experience this kind of *chesed*. One of our core strengths is that we attract students with varied backgrounds from all across the world – from Morocco to Miami, Panama to Peoria, Los Angeles to Lawrence. The fact that each student is choosing to spend his or her undergraduate years with Torah studies as a key part of the curriculum creates a self-selected unifying element across the student body. But within that group lies much diversity from which one can distinguish differences and grow. To experience this, all you need to do is extend yourself in kindness, view each fellow student as someone who was also created *be-tzelem Elokim*, and appreciate their inherent goodness.

When I was in Yeshiva as a student, I sat in the *beit midrash* next to a fellow student who really did not want to be at YU. He did not personally believe in YU's philosophy. He preferred to study in a more "right-wing" yeshiva and was only at YU because his parents forced him to attend. I was in Rabbi Rosensweig's *shiur*, learning with my morning *chavruta*, and over the course of the year, we became friends with our neighbor, talking about what we were learning and experiencing in our regular day-to-day life. By the end of the year, he told us that he had convinced his parents to allow him to switch out of YU. But sitting next to us throughout the year gave him an appreciation of YU's worldview and philosophy. We did not argue with him or convince him with "proofs." We just saw him and interacted with him as a friend. The effect of friendship flows naturally.

The profound sense of connection between individuals through the medium of *chesed* is an essential part of our worldview. When we develop our *tzelem Elokim* as an expression of Torat Adam, we do not do it simply for self-actualization; we do it for others. We are each deeply and inherently connected to one another through the virtue of kindness.

To borrow once again from the Rav's archetypes of Adam I and Adam II, the Adam of Genesis I was created with his partner;

the first human was a dyad rather than an individual. Primordial man was born connected to someone else.

As a result of this kind of creation, Adam I did not define himself, as we so often do, in contrast to someone else. His was a communitarian notion of personal identity; our personalities and identities are shaped by our relationships to others, which, in turn, create inherent responsibilities. Adam I, by being born with someone else, was born into a relationship, into a family, into a community of two. Adam II, the person who is aware of his existential reality as someone truly alone, emerged, according to the Rav, only later, in the second chapter. It is the exact opposite of what we might expect – namely, that we are first created alone and only later enjoy the company of others. In the Rav's reading, we are created first with the other, and only then do we become aware of our solitude.

In between the two categories of *yachid* (individual) and *tzibbur* (the community) are the relationships you cultivate with those closest to you: your family, friends, and, when the time is right, your spouse. They are not exactly a *tzibbur* in a technical sense. The kindness you do for them also emerges from וְאָהַבְתָּ לְרֵעֲךָ כָּמוֹךָ, the *mitzva* to love another as yourself. The moment you are more than one, you are a community of love.

In my experience, this element of *chesed* is one of the core characteristics of YU students. There is a standard here of *menschlichkeit* and goodness. From our everyday interactions to the way we conduct ourselves in the workplace and to our leadership roles in the community, people associate YU students with a certain kind of person, one who embodies *chesed*.

Every day, in the paragraph beginning with "*Sim shalom*" at the end of the *Amida*, we ask Hashem to grant peace, goodness, and blessing to all of Israel, noting that Hashem has given us a תּוֹרַת חַיִּים וְאַהֲבַת חֶסֶד. I regard this as a mandate not only to love doing *chesed,* but also to root the *chesed* we do in love. I hope that you experience this kind of love and goodness and that you always pass it on.

B'vracha,
Ari Berman

Letter #14

To Redeem the World: Torat Tzion

My Dear Student,

We have been making our way through our five core values and have finally arrived at the last and, from an individual and national perspective, the one that asks us to consider our mission. Why are we here? What is our purpose?

Through all traditional Jewish sources, the answer is clear: to help bring redemption. It is one of the questions Rava tells us we will be asked when we reflect upon our lives. Redemption is both for the Jewish people and for the world. As Yeshayahu teaches, the ultimate goal is that בֵּיתִי בֵּית תְּפִלָּה יִקָּרֵא לְכָל הָעַמִּים, "My house will be called a house of prayer for *all* peoples" (*Yeshayahu* 56:7). Torat Tzion inspires us to see ourselves as part of this grand story of redemption and to work to realize God's grand plan for the Jewish people and the world.

While this has always been true throughout Jewish history, we live today in a particular time period in which we can view ourselves as closer to realizing this majestic vision than in any other historic epoch since the exile after the destruction of the Temples. We see the hand of God in history. We recognize the great blessing Hashem bestowed in returning our people to Israel after close to two thousand years of exile. We appreciate the miraculous victories that enabled our people to regain sovereignty over our homeland, protected by a Jewish army in the Jewish state. We understand that living in a time of רֵאשִׁית צְמִיחַת גְּאֻלָּתֵנוּ, the beginning of the flourishing of the redemption, does not give us any guarantees but offers us enormous opportunities to realize our mission in the world.

And the question that beckons all of us is: What are we doing to help realize our individual and collective purpose in relation to this modern miracle?

Rambam includes redemption as one of his thirteen principles of belief as summarized in our prayer books at the end of morning services: אֲנִי מַאֲמִין בֶּאֱמוּנָה שְׁלֵמָה בְּבִיאַת הַמָּשִׁיחַ. וְאַף עַל פִּי שֶׁיִּתְמַהְמֵהַּ עִם כָּל זֶה אֲחַכֶּה לוֹ בְּכָל יוֹם שֶׁיָּבוֹא, "I believe with complete faith in the coming of the Messiah, and although he may tarry, nevertheless, I wait every day for his arrival." Rambam's principles were summarized in the first person, personalizing these articles of belief and securing them as foundational to our thinking. We are charged with believing in a better future every day, but when it comes to our role, Rambam tells us to wait for better times. In Hebrew, we recite אֲחַכֶּה לוֹ, "I will wait." This formulation asks us to have both faith and infinite patience.

We should not be waiting for tomorrow but making tomorrow.

How do we do work toward this redemption? One way, the most obvious way, is to make *aliya*, to strengthen Israel by living in the Jewish state and to work there to build the kind of model society invoked by our prophets. There has been no better time in the past two thousand years for Jews to move to, and live in, Israel. After a long and often bitter exile, we can stop our wandering and finally return to our homeland. The benefits of living in a country whose cultural context is Judaism and whose language, calendar, and culture all draw from the wellsprings of our heritage are self-evident. Jews of Babylonia, of medieval Ashkenaz, or of nineteenth-century Syria never had this option. No Jew in Auschwitz could even have imagined it.

Yeshiva University, as a religious-Zionist campus, encourages our students to make *aliya* and is committed to a full YU presence in Israel. We are creating more opportunities for our students to experience, study, and work in Israel before, during, and after college with new undergraduate and graduate programs.

Of course, even those who live in the Diaspora should devote time and resources toward strengthening Israel. Wherever you reside, we encourage you to be an active supporter and partner in Israel's flourishing. This is in part what it means to be a religious Zionist today.

But that is not the only way we express our religious Zionism in the Diaspora. We envision Jews in the Diaspora as unique contributors to the broader story of redemption, far beyond their individual contributions to Israel. By consciously and intentionally acting in a way that spreads our values and sanctifies God's name, Jews in the Diaspora are involved in the process of moving history forward.

In fact, Jews in the Diaspora community today are able to model Jewish values and influence society in ways almost unimaginable in history. I see this every day as president of Yeshiva University. Our students graduate into all levels of success, with access to all levels of power and influence. Every interaction with a colleague or doorman, every compliment to an employee or coworker, every act of integrity and kindness, is a moment of potential *kiddush*

Hashem. As such, we have an enormous opportunity to exemplify, present, and communicate our values to both the broader Jewish people and the nations of the world. The Torah, its ideas and values, are our wisdom and our truth, and our community is uniquely positioned to project that truth and be its exemplars. Tzion, redemption, unfolds when we embody and spread the ethical teachings and values sourced in the Torah to influence the world around us.

This sense of history supplies a moral dimension to our efforts to promote your spiritual and ethical development, as well as your professional success, which in most cases is in areas that directly improve society by helping others, advancing knowledge, increasing productivity, and growing the economy. All of your efforts should be contextualized within the greater project of bringing redemption, of repairing, improving, and perfecting the world.

The establishment of the State of Israel was an inflection point in Jewish history which signaled a shift in our capacity to fulfill the Jewish mission of redemption. Every one of us, all across the world, must be a partner in that mission. It should inspire us in every facet of our lives.

Every moment of our lives can be an expression of Torat Tzion if we fill our lives with this sense of meaning and purpose, if we are prepared to see the world's brokenness and work to fix it. We are not waiting for redemption. We are anticipating it, working for it.

Let us not forget that we are not accidents of history. We are drivers of history.

B'vracha,
Ari Berman

The Voice of My Beloved Is Knocking on the Door

My Dear Student,

After making *aliya* and raising my children in Israel, I have seen firsthand the benefits of infusing one's life with the spirit of Torat Tzion.

I remember when I first returned to the States to discuss a future at YU. As part of my research, I looked through the ads that YU was publishing. One of them struck a discordant note with me. It read: "Sacrifice Nothing, Achieve Everything. Yeshiva University." While the intention was to emphasize YU's unparalleled combination of academics and religious life, the implication was that it's better to live a life without sacrifice. But making sacrifices is part of a life of meaning.

Living in Israel, I saw firsthand the willingness to sacrifice everything. My son at the time was serving in a combat unit in the IDF, and he and his friends were willing to serve, despite the risks and potential personal sacrifices, for the greater good of the Jewish people.

Upon reflection, I realized that there was a key difference between the religious Zionist community in Israel and our parallel one in the United States. The history of the American Jewish community certainly includes great sacrifices to preserve our tradition, and today we can see the result of those efforts in our communal growth. We raise our children to learn Torah, observe the *mitzvot*, contribute to their communities, and raise their children to do the same. These are indeed significant achievements, and our communities have much to be proud of. In a complex world filled with great challenges to traditional communities, these are noble and essential goals.

But the overarching motion that describes our ambitions is circular and cyclical. We raise one generation to replace the next in order to raise the next generation to replace the previous one. In the religious Zionist community in Israel, by contrast, the primary movement is not circular but forward. In principle, there is a belief that their work to advance Israel is helping move history forward toward redemption. They too teach their children to learn Torah, observe the *mitzvot*, and continue the tradition, but they do so within a historical context in which they are actively responsible for the Jewish future. This enables them to frame even the greatest sacrifices as part of a larger unfolding of the majestic Jewish story.

Here in America, we too must see ourselves as part of this project. Our goal is not simply to survive, but to be partners in the great project of bringing redemption. When people do not feel themselves part of something larger, they may vote with their feet. This can bring about disengagement and attrition.

We know that something miraculous happened in 1948 with the birth of the State of Israel, and we can readily see how the flourishing of the State of Israel and the ingathering of the exiles from around the world charge us to respond to the call of history.

Rabbi Soloveitchik famously wrote that the creation of the State of Israel parallels the verses in *Shir Ha-Shirim* in which the male paramour knocks on his beloved's door, asking her to let him in. God, Rabbi Soloveitchik, explains, is knocking on the door of the Jewish people with the creation of the State of Israel. The question for us is: How do we respond?

At one point after I made *aliya*, I returned to the United States for Shabbat and heard a prominent senior pulpit rabbi tell his congregation that he is a hypocrite because he preaches the importance of Israel but has not left his congregation to go move there. This rabbi's orientation offers a narrow frame of reference to the historical opportunity that Israel presents to us, leaving us with a binary choice: Either do the "right thing" and move to Israel, or fail to rise to the moment and stay in the Diaspora. For the Diaspora religious Zionist community, this leads either to crippling guilt or cognitive dissonance. Cognitive dissonance is holding inconsistent thoughts and beliefs – for example, when one pretends to live an authentic religious life but deep down believes that they are not. It is very hard to carry a lie. Your whole religious life is in danger of becoming numb.

A broader notion of Torat Tzion, however, creates a more authentic religious life that is healing. It infuses the totality of a religious life with the spirit and purpose of bringing redemption both for those who live in Israel *and* for those who live in the Diaspora. Torat Tzion teaches us that as Jews, we all have one common, overarching goal, and that is to redeem the world and transform it for the better, to bring our sacred values out into the world, to birth a world suffused by justice, goodness, prosperity, and transcendence. This can and should happen regardless of location.

There are very significant challenges in our community and society today. For the Jewish people, threats like antisemitism and assimilation are on the rise. As a society, we are struggling with the aftereffects of a global pandemic, a polarized political climate, and major shifts in technology whose social repercussions we still do not fully comprehend. But with all of the challenges, please remember, my dear student, that we are living in an era that is also miraculous and wondrous. The Jewish people are no longer lost in exile. We have once again returned to our homeland. Torah study is open and accessible throughout the world. Jews are free to live by the teachings of our heritage and by the tenets of our faith. Where once we might have looked at our neighbors and saw only oppressors, today we see them as potential partners. This presents us with not only great opportunities, but also great responsibilities.

Wherever God takes you in this world, know that you can and must play a role in the sacred mission of the Jewish people. God is knocking on our door.

It's time to let God in.

B'vracha,
Ari Berman

Letter #16

The Life to Which You Were Born and the Life You Choose

My Dear Student,

Torat Emet, Torat Adam, Torat Chaim, Torat Chesed, and Torat Tzion.

Seek truth. Discover your sacred potential. Live your values. Act with compassion. And bring redemption.

These are our core Torah values. They fill out and enhance the foundation of Torah U-Madda.

These values differentiate us. Taken as a whole, they constitute a layered notion of personal identity and purpose. Let me illustrate with my own personal story.

Cyla Fenster ("Bubbe"), my wife's grandmother, is one of my heroines. She was born in Poland and had a large family, including her brother Pinchas, to whom she was very close. Her childhood sweetheart, Shlomo, eventually became her husband, and together they lived a relatively quiet and peaceful life. But then the Nazis invaded Poland, entered their town, and gathered and killed all of its Jews, except for the few who escaped.

Bubbe managed to escape into the woods with Shlomo and a few of their nephews and nieces, but no one else in their large family was as fortunate. Her sweet brother Pinchas became a sad memory. Bubbe never left her husband's side, and together they managed to evade the Germans. They eventually found their way to Romania. Following the war, they left Europe and went to Cuba. When Castro rose to power, they fled once again, this time to New York.

The story of the Jews is a story of movement, adaptation, and change. These too are ingredients of redemption – a fierce resilience and commitment to life and Jewish continuity, no matter the circumstances.

Several decades later, Bubbe received a call from a friend of hers who had just returned from a trip to the Soviet Union. "Cyla" she said, "you need to sit down. I have something astounding to tell you. Your brother, Pinchas – he is alive. While you ran west, he escaped east. You each thought the other was dead, but Pinchas is alive and living in Russia."

Can you imagine hearing such news, thinking your sibling did not survive and then hearing so many years later that he did?

Bubbe immediately contacted Pinchas, but they were never able to meet in person. Sadly, not long after, Pinchas died, and they never had a family reunion. But Pinchas had a daughter named Gala, who married Vladimir. When they had a son, they named him Pinchas, after her father. After the Iron Curtain fell, Gala and her family moved to Israel.

Not long after, Anita and I were in Israel, where I was learning at YU's Gruss Kollel. At the end of the year, Anita gave birth to our first son, whom we named Shlomo after her grandfather, who had recently passed away. Bubbe came to Israel for the *brit*. I vividly remember how she was sitting with her new great-grandson, Shlomo, on her lap, when in walked a woman who had a clear family resemblance. It was her niece Gala, whom she had never previously met.

Gala came holding the hand of a little boy named Pinchas. When Pinchas ran over to see the baby, once again Bubbe was surrounded by a Pinchas and a Shlomo. At this event, when we welcomed our first son into Hashem's covenant, we saw with our own eyes the way God's miracles persist in our day.

The Nazis thought they could kill us, remove every last one of us from the earth. But they could not. We survived. We will always survive. This is the divine covenantal promise. And even more, we returned to our homeland. Pinchas and Shlomo were alive again, and this time they connected with each other in Jerusalem, the capital of the modern Jewish State of Israel.

Bubbe's life represents the dramatic story of the Jewish people in the modern era, a story of an indomitable spirit able to transcend destruction and to rebuild a lost world. And the story continues. At my investiture as president of this university, Bubbe attended and watched with pride. She was over one hundred years old at the time, surrounded by generations of her family and sitting next to my daughter Tamar, who inherited her great-grandmother's inner strength and personal kindness. In my investiture remarks, I shared Bubbe's story, because it is now part of my story as well. Acknowledging her presence that day brought the standing ovation that her incredible Jewish journey deserved.

But this story is not over. One of the most significant moments of my life was when Anita and I brought our oldest son, Shlomo, to the army base to officially enlist in the IDF. It was very emotional for me as a father. As I stood there with him, I watched young men and women signing up for their different army units singing and dancing in a circle. This was not a sad day for them. It was a day of celebration. It was apparent that they saw their service to the country as a privilege.

When Shlomo came back for his first Shabbat at home in uniform, I was deeply proud of him and proud that we brought into the world someone who would be part of the great Jewish story in the State of Israel. He represented a new chapter for our family.

Shlomo served in an intelligence unit. Our second son, Yehuda, was in a combat unit. Anyone in the army sacrifices years and faces challenges that can be potentially corrosive to one's faith and observance, but in combat, the sacrifice is even greater. When you enter a combat unit, you have to prepare yourself physically and mentally for every eventuality. You prepare for the worst and hope for the best.

For me, this recognition was profound, frightening, and inspiring. My wife and I raised our children to embrace service, and then when the moment came, I suddenly experienced the very real physical fear of what this could mean. We were joining with tens of thousands of other Israeli families who had come face-to-face with the reality of army service for generations. Many of them have stood before coffins draped in blue and white flags. They weep every year on Mount Herzl.

I remember so clearly the Shabbat before Yehuda went into the army. We were sitting in shul, and it came time for *Birkat Kohanim*, the priestly blessing. I put my *tallit* over my head and my son's head to protect him spiritually. And I was crying. I said to him, "All my life, Yehuda, all I've ever wanted is to put my *tallit* over your head and protect you. And now, you're going out, and you're going to protect me."

It was a meaningful and defining moment for me as a father and as a Jew. But you don't have to move to Israel or join the army to see your life as one of service. Sadly, communal or public service is not normative, especially not for college students in American universities. Inducting our sons into the Israeli army made me reflect, when I came back to the United States, on one of the problems of a society focused almost exclusively on the self. What happens to people who sacrifice nothing to achieve everything?

This is where all of our core values do their hardest work. Torat Emet teaches us to be honest with ourselves about public and religious service. Torat Adam helps us find ourselves by finding ourselves to something greater than ourselves. Torat Chaim helps us integrate what we learn with the best way to love. Torat Chesed reminds us to have others at the top of our minds and hearts. Torat Tzion brings all these values together to move history forward.

So where and when did your story start and where will it end? How will it continue? We sometimes think our stories begin at birth and end at death, but in the Jewish tradition, it is far more expansive. My personal story includes my origins. I am my parents' son and my grandparents' grandson. And once I met and married Anita, my heart expanded and we forged a new unit, and my back story expanded as well to include the stories of her parents and grandparents. And after we are gone, our children and, with God's help, our future grandchildren will continue all of our stories.

Shlomo was a child in Poland. Shlomo was a husband and a survivor. Shlomo was also raised in America and immigrated to Israel and served in the IDF. It's all part of the same story.

This is the lesson of the five core Torah values. The story of the Jewish people – all of our stories – begins at Sinai. It begins with the Torah. It begins with Truth. Our stories do not end after our 120 years, but at Tzion, when we reach redemption. What we do in our years on this earth is develop ourselves, our Torat Adam. We live lives of *mitzvot*, filled with *chesed*, working to spread our values and redeem the world.

Jews are directed by our tradition to develop both their personal way of serving God as well as to locate their individual stories within the context of the broader narrative of the Jewish people. Rabbi Soloveitchik famously distinguished between two covenants. The covenant of fate relates to the historical events that will befall the Jewish people, while the covenant of destiny refers to the choice of living an elevated life of Torah and *mitzvot*. Our tradition directs us to develop ourselves in both ways, combining history with heritage, fate with destiny.

The way in which each of you blend these values will naturally shift depending on your proclivities and the different time periods of your life. Collectively, though, they root us deeply within a structured value system and provide moral guidance and direction for living our lives. They propel us to develop our talents and skills while directing us to reach outward and connect to others in kindness. And they inspire us with a grand, historic purpose to make a difference and impact the world.

This is what we believe Judaism represents and what God wants from all of us. Life is for service. No matter what you do in the future, think of how your personal choices serve others. Perhaps you will consider Jewish education or the rabbinate as your service. In our Yeshiva University family, this is one of the highest levels of service. It offers, as I have found, a future of meaning and impact. It is sacred and important. But remember: No matter who you are and what your gifts lead you to do, your purpose is to be of service to your family, to your community, to your people, and to the world.

This joins you to the covenant of destiny.

B'vracha,
Ari Berman

Letter #17

What's in a Name?

My Dear Student,

Now that we have a more descriptive sense of our five core Torah values, it is very clear that we have a language problem. And I need your help to solve it.

We use a lot of labels within Judaism, and they are important because they help us understand who we are. But religious taxonomies also limit us and often fail to fully capture our reality and the nuanced nature of our commitments.

Take, for example, the words we currently use to describe segments of the Ashkenazic Jewish population. The terms Reform, Conservative, and Orthodox were phrases coined for denominations developed largely in the nineteenth and twentieth centuries. Call it the impact of postmodernism, call it the passage of time, but these labels are increasingly losing their original meanings and force. While there are still synagogues, rabbinical seminaries, and youth organizations associated with these movements, these do not appear to be compelling ways of thinking about Judaism in North America today.

Looking ahead, demographic polls indicate that these terms will likely write themselves out of history. The story these polls are telling is that the two categories of growth in the Diaspora in the next thirty to forty years will be the Orthodox and the unaffiliated. The latter term is often used in research, as well as "nones," to refer to Jews and others for whom Judaism plays little or no role in their construction of identity. Through nonmembership, high intermarriage rates, and weak or no Jewish education, many Jews – without a real injection of Jewish meaning – will cease to find in Judaism a marker of who they are.

The words "affiliated" and "unaffiliated" are largely measures of belonging, relevant to nonprofit organizations and houses of worship, but "doing Jewish" today for many Jews does not involve any of these labels or rubrics. You can find personal Jewish meaning in rituals, study, and community while not being a member of any formal structure. The terms are less relevant and less descriptive of who we are now. The dividing lines are blurred for some and not at all relevant for others.

The number of Jews who identify as Orthodox is on the rise in contemporary sociological studies that once upon a time predicted its demise. It seems that Judaism in the Diaspora will become either a very superficial ethnic identity or one that indicates a deep and lifelong commitment.

Although we should approach demographic studies with some skepticism – we have, after all, outlived predictions of Jewish demise for centuries – we can see the patterns playing out already. The question of the future, and some may argue, the present, will not be what denomination you belong to, but whether or not you are serious about Judaism, in whichever way you practice it.

Within Orthodoxy, we also use language that can be misleading. While you're here and throughout your life, you will hear certain words describing Orthodoxy today: Open Orthodoxy, Modern Orthodoxy, Centrist Orthodoxy, YU *machmir*, Ultra-Orthodoxy, Neo-Chasidic, Charedi, and Right-Wing Judaism. There are probably more labels that I don't know. You may find that one of these labels suits you, or you might feel unsure where you belong. Maybe none of these words really describes you. Or maybe you don't want to be pigeonholed into any category.

One glaring challenge is in our choice of language to describe our religious commitments. Phrases like Modern Orthodox are wanting. Ask a group of people to describe the ideology of Modern Orthodoxy, and you'll likely get a host of different answers, even on this campus. And the label carries questionable and false implications. "Modern" implies that our view of Judaism, which balances a full set of Torah values while embracing and contributing to society, is new. It's actually very old, dating all the way back to Sinai. In addition, Modern and Ultra-Orthodox are generally seen as measures relative to each other rather than understood on their own terms, as if Orthodoxy were placed on a linear spectrum in which there is a "less and more" paradigm. Ultra-Orthodoxy in this range is more. Modern Orthodoxy is less. In such a model, students who are passionate about their Judaism might mistakenly assume that their Modern Orthodox community is "less than" that of the Ultra-Orthodox, who are the real deal, uncompromising and true. While labels may be helpful for outsiders, their superficiality creates deep problems and dramatic distortions for insiders.

A more accurate description of our thinking is cited in the name of Rabbi Chaim Soloveitchik. When the two Jewish values of saving a life and keeping Shabbat were in conflict, he was not *meikel* (lenient) about the laws of Shabbat, he famously said, but *machmir* (stringent) about the laws of saving lives. What he was highlighting is that there are a multitude of Torah values, and the correct Torah orientation is one that upholds and honors all of these values. It is a maximalist view of a Torah commitment.

Specific circumstances will require you to choose how to navigate competing values at a moment in time. But even in such cases, the other values do not disappear, nor are they necessarily less important. When saving a life competes with the laws of Shabbat, one will need to choose what to do, but both life and Shabbat remain holy and precious. Highlighting this point is that given a slight shift of circumstances, such as a changed level of risk, one might reassess and arrive at a different conclusion. It is precisely our range of values and our commitment to that range that allows us to respond to an ever-changing world with the confidence that Halacha can address whatever dilemmas we may confront with sensitivity.

Within this perspective, Torah Judaism advocates many different values. Our most central and pressing life issues are rarely a case of simply doing more than or doing less than, being more than or being less than. When we do what we perceive is "more," it often comes at the sacrifice of another, equally compelling value.

If, for example, your religious quest leads you to a place of greater isolation and separation, with greater borders and boundaries between you and the rest of the society, you sacrifice your ability to shape, influence, and lead in that society. If you place yourself in a fortress to shield yourself from negative influences, you will also be less capable of bringing Torah to the rest of the Jewish people and to the world.

But, by the same token, if you're out in the world without a sophisticated filtration system, and if you don't think about protecting and shielding yourself from negative influences, you are putting yourself at significant risk to lose the strength of your commitment. Here too you will not be able to lead and influence. Rabbi Saadia Gaon, in his introduction to *Emunot Ve-De'ot,* compares exposing one's faith to pernicious influences to going out in extremes of temperature without adequate protection. We would not do that to our bodies, nor should we do it to our souls.

At YU, we provide you with the skills, tools, and role models to deepen the threshold of intensity when it comes to your learning and Torah observance, while at the same time empowering you to go out into the world as beacons of light who will make important contributions as citizens.

Life questions such as what community you should live in or what literature you read are not "more or less" issues. They involve balancing priorities and calibrating them with the consciousness that the Torah demands us to uphold a multiplicity of values. One of our educational goals at Yeshiva is to help students prioritize their values and live by them.

Unfortunately, many people still talk about YU as if we were in the sixties and seventies, using language and ideas that do not resonate with an emerging generation of students. Even more problematic is that these labels at times create unnecessary divisions. The labels of "Modern" and "Centrist" Orthodoxy are terminologies and outmoded frameworks that diminish the kind of thinking we need for the twenty-first century.

I am not sure what language we should be using to describe the kind of Judaism we promote at YU. In Israel, the term *Dati Leumi* literally means "National Religious" and has political overtones. As we are religious Zionists, maybe a more apt phrase is *Torani Tzioni*, as it communicates our commitment to Torah, Israel, and redemption. I am also partial to "Torah Judaism," as our educational philosophy comprises the full complement of Torah values. I am struggling to find the right words to describe a Judaism – not a denomination – that is rich in *mitzvot*, study, ethics, *tefilla*, piety, and *chesed*, while engaging with the larger world in the quest to bring redemption. Our objective is to sanctify God's name in the world, in the spirit of Yeshayahu's prophecy, which is impossible to do if we don't engage with the world.

We need to wrap our language around *our* values. But instead, we use limited descriptions of ourselves that invite weak and often meaningless comparisons with the practice and beliefs of other Jews.

One thing is clear. We need a new lexicon for today's new dilemmas that stays true to our ancient wisdom. As the emerging generation of committed Jews, this will largely be your work – to find the words and the language to describe the Judaism of the future, one that is deeply engaging and inspiring, demanding and loving.

I encourage you to engage in that conversation and help me, help us, discover the language of the present and future.

B'vracha,
Ari Berman

Strategies for a Life Well Lived

My Dear Student,

There will inevitably be times when treasured values will clash with each other. *Emet*, honesty, often clashes with *shalom*, peace. Individual needs will conflict with those of one's broader community. How does one navigate such moments of tension? How does one prioritize when pushed to choose between competing values?

While each specific instance would require its own analysis, there are three basic strategies that I will share that help me when I face such crossroads.

The first is captured by Rabbi Lamm in an article on his reflections on "Peace and Truth." Rabbi Lamm describes a notion of complementarity in which

> neither peace or truth need be given second billing.... We affirm both, attempting whenever possible to conform to

each of this polarity. Where choices must be made, we choose now one, now the other, depending on the circumstances and judgment...but always remembering that the other pole remains vital and relevant and may not be overlooked.

When values clash, we need to make choices, but it's not that one value is necessarily more important than another. It may simply be that different circumstances require different responses. One value may take prominence for a time, but the other value does not disappear. If circumstances change, the other value may rise in importance. Oftentimes, disagreements about how to respond to a particular issue are not debates about core values themselves, but rather disagreements about how to apply our shared set of values to specific circumstances.

To my mind, a great example of this is found in one of our foundational stories in *Bereshit*. When Hashem calls to Avraham to issue the directive to make the ultimate sacrifice, Avraham's response is simple. He says, "*Hineni*" – God, I am here (*Bereshit* 22:1). *Hineni*, as explained by Rashi, does not simply mean "I am present"; it means "I am here for You," to do whatever You need me to do. And this, of course, is the ultimate value for Avraham *ha-Ivri* – to follow God in all ways.

Interestingly, later on in the story, when Yitzchak calls out, "Father, father," Avraham once again responds, "*Hineni*" – I am here for you (*Bereshit* 22:7). This reflects a second aspect of Avraham, not Avraham the "*Ivri*," but Avraham the "*Avi*." Avraham also values his love, paternal care, and devotion to his son Yitzchak. Avraham's whole life was spent praying for and then protecting Yitzchak from any harm. The Torah, by employing the same word *hineni* in both circumstances, uncovers the inexorable tension that Avraham was feeling at this moment. Avraham is both servant of God and caretaker of his son.

Avraham would do anything for either of them. But now he is faced with a decision in which he needs to choose one aspect of his life over another. When Avraham decides to follow God's command, he is sacrificing not only Yitzchak, but also a part of himself. The Avraham *"Avi"* is being sacrificed by the Avraham *"Ivri."*

With this background, we can better understand the resolution of this dilemma. At the end of the story, the angel stays Avraham's hand by calling his name twice: "Avraham, Avraham." And Avraham once again answers, *"Hineni"* (*Bereshit* 22:11). Why mention Avraham twice? God ultimately does *not* want Avraham to sacrifice his son. But God also requires Avraham to be responsive to the greater call of faith. God accepts and desires both sides of Avraham, the *Ivri* and the *Avi*. The chapter begins with these two callings in conflict but resolves them with Avraham able to respond in fullness to both callings – the worshipper and the father.

When Avraham responds the third time with *Hineni*, he is finally able to understand the inherent value of the multiple callings in his own life. Each of them makes demands. Each of them speaks to profound and important aspects of his soul. Sometimes those demands are in conflict. With his last *Hineni*, Avraham expresses his willingness to respond to more than one calling.

Your lives will ask you to respond to different and competing callings. They may take the form of a major life decision, like choosing a career path that is better suited to you or one that focuses on the community as a whole. These conflicts may appear in your domestic lives as parents, such as deciding what to do on an evening when your child asks for your attention, but your work or religious obligations are pressing. The story of Avraham teaches us that if you're always saying *Hineni* to one kind of commitment, choosing one value over another, you're probably making a mistake. God wants you to uphold and balance a multitude of commitments in order to live an authentic religious life as a true *eved Hashem* (servant of God).

The first strategy is finding a way to balance and blend a multitude of values in your life. I do not want to minimize how difficult this is. We are all juggling many competing values. What they don't tell you when you juggle is that some of the balls are made out of glass. You have to prioritize that which really matters when seeking balance.

The second strategy is to take into account your specific personality, character traits, and circumstances. Because Halacha is the determining structure for Orthodox Jewish life, we often use terms associated with Halacha to talk about life. Take, for example, the terms *"lechatchila"* and *"bedieved."* There is a maximal way to do something when all conditions are ideal, and there is a way to satisfy one's basic obligations when circumstances are not perfect.

As an aspiration, we should all try to be maximalist Jews and root out mediocrity when it comes to our religious observance. But oftentimes, when it comes to life decisions, we cannot consistently be governed by the same categories, because life itself is *bedieved.* It's never ideal. It's making the best out of the circumstances we find ourselves in and making good choices under often suboptimal conditions. Moreover, so much of life is filled with areas in which there is no clear right or wrong. The determining factor is what's right for that specific area and what's right for *you.*

When it comes to conceptual Halacha, we strive for pristine ideals. When it comes to personal life choices, we place those ideals within the context of real-life situations and harness our self-knowledge.

Take, for example, the major questions you will face in life: Whom will you marry? Where will you live? What will you choose for a career? By definition, these kinds of questions are very different from those that apply to particular *mitzvot*, such as lighting Shabbat candles or putting on *tefillin.* Most of the *mitzvot* we perform regularly are *chiyuvim*, legal obligations. But a larger question like our future place of residence, according to most halachic decisors who do not regard living in Israel as a legal obligation, is not an obligation – a *chiyuv* – but a life choice. Similarly, there are limited halachic discussions about what profession to enter or the parameters of that profession, and there are broad halachic guidelines about whom to marry. But we are not to make these choices based on disembodied, decontextualized sources. We have to take into account our backgrounds, skills, talents, needs, and desires.

Such life decisions are not *"chiyuvim"* but *"kiyumim,"* not obligations but states of being that induce a healthier, more authentic way of living. On a piece of paper, we might come to the conclusion that the most sacred life choice is to be an educator or a rabbi, but that piece of paper is merely two-dimensional. Life is three-dimensional. Your abilities and predilections might point you to different choices. In these areas of life, it's about who you are, rather than what you think you should or need to do because of someone else's expectations.

This also explains why the Mishna (*Pe'ah* 1:1) says there is no minimum or maximum measure – a *shiur* – for certain acts of kindness. Rambam (*Hilchot Avel* 14:1) explains that the *mitzva* to love one's fellow as oneself means that one should visit the sick, accompany the dead, and share joy with the bride and groom. But there is no one way or one appropriate measure to accomplish any of these acts. That depends on the person doing them.

Although there are no limits to these commandments, there are what I like to call *"mitzva* consequences" that should impact our life choices. Our friends can enhance our performance of *mitzvot* or detract from them. Our choice of profession can leave time for family and the fulfillment of *shemirat ha-mitzvot* or not. Our choice of spouse and community will also have significant *mitzva* consequences. Our hobbies and how we spend our recreational time can also have *mitzva* consequences.

We make choices that reflect our personalities, needs, and drives, and they also each have consequences. As you think about the major life decisions ahead of you, please consider who you are in the picture. This awareness will not only help you make better decisions, but also promote respect for the choices others make. Just as your decisions are deeply personal, so are the decisions of others. Respecting others and avoiding being judgmental creates healthier relationships and a more productive society. All this comes from the deeper appreciation of the primacy of the individual in making life choices.

The third strategy is to surround yourself with people who will support you, care about you, and help you through life. The Mishna in *Avot* (1:6) states, עֲשֵׂה לְךָ רַב, וּקְנֵה לְךָ חָבֵר, "Make for yourself a rabbi and acquire for yourself a friend." This teaching calls for an active investment on your part to develop those relationships.

One of the great blessings in my life has been having great teachers. In them I have found models of truth, integrity, courage, devotion, kindness, and love.

When I was growing up, I sat in the same row as my uncle, Rabbi Julius Berman, during Shabbat *davening*. I watched not only how he *davened*, learned, and taught Torah weekly in shul, but how he conducted himself with his neighbors and friends who sought his advice about personal and communal matters. Throughout every stage of my life, he encouraged me and guided me, serving as a role model for compassionate, forward-thinking Jewish communal leadership on the highest level.

Rabbi Michael Rosensweig's incredible erudition and creativity in all areas of Torah, as well as history, literature, and philosophy, informed and shaped my intellectual and spiritual life. His brilliance that is on regular display to his students is only matched by the kindness and care he shows to each individual student. He invited my participation not only in his classroom, but in our lifelong ongoing dialogue, from which I continue to be nourished.

Rabbi Jacob J. Schacter brought me into his shul and brought me into his heart. Serving as his intern, assistant, and associate at The Jewish Center for six years gave me a front-row seat to witness not only a rabbi at the top of his profession, but an *eved Hashem* par excellence whose profound sensitivity and kindness to others elevated every interaction with congregants, communal leaders, and neighbors, Jews and non-Jews alike. When I started my tenure, Rabbi Schacter put his arm around me to extend his support, and throughout every stage of my life since, even when few others were present, he consistently and unwaveringly was a primary source of strength and wisdom.

Rabbi Aharon Lichtenstein's photograph is on my desk. He is my *rebbi,* and although he's no longer alive, I consciously use the present tense, as I still seek his guidance and hear his voice when I face complex situations and decisions. Since my days as a student in his yeshiva, I would regularly turn to him for all matters of personal advice. Sometimes just being in his presence was clarifying. There were times when I would come to him for guidance about a significant life decision, with all of my justifications and machinations in my head, but I found myself unable to even utter them in front of him. He was such an *ish emet,* a person of truth, that all matters of artifice and self-deception would naturally fall away in his presence. Other times, Rabbi Lichtenstein would generously share personal stories and life lessons he learned not only from the texts that he assiduously studied, but from the context of a life well lived.

Rabbi Lichtenstein was with me for my entire adult life. He was the *sandek* at my son's *brit* and participated in almost all of our family *smachot,* even when it was difficult for him because of the demands on his time. I know it inconvenienced him at times, but he never said so. He showed by example the importance of the *rebbi-talmid* relationship simply by being present on occasions that mattered to me.

I share these stories with you, my student, to highlight the impact a true teacher will have on your life. Such a teacher not only imparts deep wisdom to you and provides great emotional support, but also serves as a living example for navigating a real life of commitment to Torah and our values. Everyone's life is filled with complexity and moments of decision in which values clash. Watching those who embody the highest ideals make their life decisions and hearing from them their stories and advice are great vehicles for you to learn how to apply our values to your life decisions.

It is interesting that the Mishna in *Avot* links the directive to make yourself a teacher with the one to acquire a friend. For friendships are the other relationships that will provide you with the strength to make hard decisions and help you believe in yourself and find your authentic voice within the tradition. True friends are those with you throughout your life, based not on your position, current title, or achievements, but on mutual respect and affection. The friends that I made in YU, in my college years and my years in *semicha*, have remained my closest friends in life. We had no idea how our lives would turn out when we were hanging out in the dorm after hours. But the connections we formed during those years were the bonds that have continued to infuse our lives with great warmth and joy.

Of course, when it comes to friends, the most important person in your life is your best friend, your spouse. In Halacha, the bond between husband and wife is singular. It is the only relationship in which there is a merging between two identities, so that two individuals also stand as one. The commitment that is represented by marriage, in which two people tie their lives and destinies to one another, is transformative. It elevates the visceral love and excitement of being together into a covenantal experience. To have one person in the world you can fully trust and with whom you lower your natural guard and share your vulnerability is true intimacy and the greatest human source of comfort and joy in life.

There is no doubt that my greatest gratitude to Hashem is for bringing Anita into my life. It is this relationship that provides me with the inner strength to navigate and find happiness throughout all of the vicissitudes and dramatic turns that life naturally brings. Our life journey, with all of its inherent challenges and joys, heartbreaks and triumphs, is made sweeter by the fact that we are traveling this road together.

My great wish for you, my dear student, is that you similarly find the friends, and the one true friend, who will accompany you through your journey.

These three strategies will help you actualize our core Torah values in your life:

1. Balancing and calibrating your values throughout your life
2. Accounting for your specific personality, character traits, and circumstances when making decisions
3. Surrounding yourself with the teachers, friends, and loved ones who will enable your best self to emerge and develop

With these strategies, you will form a strong basis upon leaving YU for a lifetime of Torah and self-discovery, purpose and joy, meaning and mission.

May life bring you much success and happiness.

Warmest regards,
Ari Berman

Becoming a Leader: A Prayer for the Journey

Dear Friend,

When we began this journey, I addressed you as a student. But as I gave you glimpses into my own life, my challenges, and my ideas, I leave you as a friend.

I share my thoughts and story with you in these letters not to generalize my experiences, but to encourage you to develop your own way of seeing the world. The Rav once wrote that a human being can only express his or her *own* feelings, with the hope that "by formulating his own experiences in clear language, others may benefit from this self-revelation and enrich their own religious life." It is my hope, dear student, that in sharing some of myself, you will try to analyze and concretize your own experiences here at Yeshiva University in your quest for an engaged, holistic spiritual and intellectual life.

In whatever way you "formulate your own experience" here, please know that I am rooting for your success. One of the first *Shabbatot* I spent in my position as president at YU was at our Beren campus with our undergraduate women. In a talk at the end of Shabbat, I mentioned to our students how important it is for us to come together as one united whole, that in a time in which competition and self-focus are the underpinnings of the society in which we live, our student body must exemplify the value of supporting one another and rooting for each other's success. I mentioned to our students that I am rooting for each of them to succeed in life. Then one young woman in the crowd shouted out, "Rabbi, we are rooting for *you!*"

I was very moved by what she said and think of that exchange often, especially when I face difficulties. I want to tell you that this is the feeling that has kept me buoyant and hopeful, even in times of challenge – that we are rooting for each other and that we are rooting for our institution's success. Your success and our collective success carry great consequences. In it lies the actualization of our most important endeavor: a Judaism that is inspired and inspiring.

There is much more to say about the values we most cherish. I hope that you will add your contributions and commentary to the five core Torah values that are the centerpiece of this book. We come from a commentary tradition, and with each of your insights you contribute to this sacred conversation across the ages. Ask yourself: Which value comes easily or naturally to me and which Torah value requires improvement? This is your life's work. It is my life's work.

It is my hope that the ideas in this book will help inspire you to reach your potential and fulfill your personal destiny. Your personal destiny is profoundly connected to the destiny of the Jewish people as a whole, and I encourage you to think of yourself in those terms. As you develop your way of serving God within the context of our ennobling tradition, consider yourself a leader and person of impact, in whatever way best suits your strengths and life circumstances – whether it's in your home and your family, your synagogue and communal work, or your office and society at large. By living and transmitting your values to this generation and the next and proudly representing what we stand for to those around you, you become a leader and a person of impact.

One of my great joys of returning to Yeshiva University at this time is to experience two of my sons, Binyamin and Yonatan, simultaneously following in my footsteps and forging their own paths. After studying in yeshiva in Israel and devoting years of service in the IDF, Binyamin is now an undergraduate on campus at YU, while Yonatan just started his first year at MTA. They are studying in the same buildings and walking in the same hallways in which I studied and walked three decades ago and in which my father studied and walked six decades ago. More significantly, they are studying the same Torah, internalizing the same values, and receiving the same *mesora*. They will each apply them differently as fitting with their personalities and life experiences, but the cycle continues from one generation to the next.

Yeshiva University is a family. It's a family that welcomes newcomers and legacy students alike. The Sages (*Sifrei, Devarim* 6:7) teach that the mandate cited in the paragraph of *Shema* to teach one's children refers also to one's students: לְבָנֶיךָ – אֵלּוּ תַּלְמִידֶיךָ. At this yeshiva, our students are as precious to us as our children, and the greatest blessing we give to our children is that they are never alone in life, but rather find comfort, joy, and love at every moment of their journey. As Rabbi Soloveitchik explained through a personal anecdote of being separated from his family when he was wheeled into surgery, there is one relationship that is with a person at every moment of his or her life. It is that relationship that sustains us, comforts us, and gives us true *simcha* in life: וּשְׂמַחְתֶּם לִפְנֵי ה' אֱלֹהֵיכֶם שִׁבְעַת יָמִים, "and you shall rejoice before your God for seven days" (*Vayikra* 23:40). True joy, according to Rabbi Soloveitchik, is when we stand in the presence of God.

I leave you, my student, with the same blessing I have given to my own children on Shabbat, at celebrations, and at moments of transition:

יְבָרֶכְךָ ה' וְיִשְׁמְרֶךָ.
יָאֵר ה' פָּנָיו אֵלֶיךָ וִיחֻנֶּךָּ.
יִשָּׂא ה' פָּנָיו אֵלֶיךָ וְיָשֵׂם לְךָ שָׁלוֹם.

May Hashem bless you and protect you!
May Hashem deal kindly and graciously with you!
May Hashem bestow His favor upon you
and grant you peace!

My blessing to you echoes the one I offered when we began this journey at the beginning of the book. It is a blessing rooted in the grand vision of the prophet Yeshayahu (42:5–7):

כֹּה אָמַר הָאֵל ה' בּוֹרֵא הַשָּׁמַיִם וְנוֹטֵיהֶם רֹקַע הָאָרֶץ וְצֶאֱצָאֶיהָ
נֹתֵן נְשָׁמָה לָעָם עָלֶיהָ וְרוּחַ לַהֹלְכִים בָּהּ.
אֲנִי ה' קְרָאתִיךָ בְצֶדֶק וְאַחְזֵק בְּיָדֶךָ וְאֶצָּרְךָ וְאֶתֶּנְךָ לִבְרִית עָם
לְאוֹר גּוֹיִם.
לִפְקֹחַ עֵינַיִם עִוְרוֹת לְהוֹצִיא מִמַּסְגֵּר אַסִּיר מִבֵּית כֶּלֶא יֹשְׁבֵי
חֹשֶׁךְ.

Thus said God the Lord, who created the heavens and stretched them out, who spread out the earth and what it brings forth, who gave breath to the people upon it and life to those who walk thereon:
I the Lord, in My grace, have summoned you, and I have grasped you by the hand. I created you and appointed you a covenant people, a light of nations.

To open eyes deprived of light, to rescue prisoners from
confinement, from the dungeon those who sit in darkness.

Yeshayahu describes our divine calling to be a light unto the world,
bringing light to all those around us. This is a wondrous vision of
our holy mission. But my favorite part of these verses is the way
Yeshayahu describes our relationship with God. I love the image
of Hashem grasping each of us by the hand.

Throughout my life, and especially in this position as president of the flagship Jewish university, I try to walk with the sense
of God's constant support, and I feel that my job is to help create
an institution whose graduates go out into the world and generate
more light. My blessing to you is that you should feel the love of
God's presence throughout all of your days and years.

As you begin and continue your studies here, may you
always radiate this holy light, treasuring your past as you create
your future. We are here for you. I am here for you. Please introduce yourself so that I can welcome you personally.

I believe we can all get an A on Rava's exam and that you've
taken one step closer to the best grade possible by joining our
Yeshiva University family.

Most importantly, may you feel that Hashem is always by
your side as you embark on this next, exciting stage of your life,
now and forever.

Shalom,
Ari Berman

Acknowledgments

While I am deeply thankful to all who participated and partnered in this process, I would like to thank a number of the key people who have significantly contributed to the ideas and to the production of this book.

Special thanks to my *rebbi*, Rabbi Dr. Michael Rosensweig, who read and commented on this book and whose Torah has nourished me throughout my life. The framework of the five core Torah values was first laid out in my conversations with him before I began my tenure as president. His influence and that of all of my primary *rabbeim* in my formative years, including Rabbi Dr. Aharon Lichtenstein *zt"l*, Rabbi Mordechai Willig, Rabbi Hershel Schachter, Rabbi Aharon Kahn, and my uncle Rabbi Julius Berman, are felt throughout the pages of this book. Rabbi Dr. Jacob J. Schacter has been an incredible mentor to me, and I am deeply grateful for his careful review of this book.

I must also acknowledge the outsized influence of Maran HaRav Yosef Dov Soloveitchik *zt"l* on these letters and on our community. Although I did not have the privilege of studying directly under the Rav, in my eyes, this formulation of our core Torah values is simply a reformulation of the Torah I studied at Yeshiva under the shadow and influence of his teachings and writings.

In addition to the influential teachers of my younger years, I am deeply thankful for the relationships I have continued to develop in my current tenure at YU. Many individuals have helped develop the themes in this book, including our Provost, Dr. Selma Botman, Rabbi Dovid Bashevkin, Judah Diament, Rabbi Yosef Kalinsky, Rabbi Dr. Ari Lamm, Rabbi Yaakov Neuburger, Rabbi Marc Penner, Dean Shoshana Schechter, Rabbi Mayer Twersky, and Dean Noam Wasserman. Thanks to Rabbi Marc Eichenbaum for his assistance with the references. And special thanks to Vice Provost Erica Brown for her advice, guidance, and support in helping me formulate and express the ideas in this volume.

I am most grateful to the many students who read this book and took the time to give me specific and general feedback on the draft version. You will notice your contributions on many of this book's pages. You are a treasure. Those of you just beginning your education here and those of you who already graduated and reflected on your experience are my ultimate readers. You offered me new ways to think about this material and to think about who we are as a yeshiva and as a university and who we can become.

May Hashem bless you all for your guidance.

Since I began my tenure as president, I have been blessed to have as my right hand and Chief of Staff Julie Schreier. Nothing I have done at YU, including this book, could have been accomplished without her. To her and to our stellar team in the Office of the President, including Yael Evgi, Ilana Lehrer, David Ashendorf, and Josh Weinstein, I am deeply thankful.

Thank you as well to Matthew Miller, publisher at Koren Jerusalem, as well as Rabbi Reuven Ziegler, Ita Olesker, Caryn

Meltz, Tani Bayer, Tomi Mager, and Debbie Ismailoff for their professionalism in working on this book and their dedication to spreading Jewish ideas throughout the world.

I am deeply honored to have my dear friends Debbie and Elliot Gibber as partners in producing this book. Their generosity, support, and extraordinary example of Jewish leadership have been a constant source of profound strength and inspiration to me personally and to the Jewish world as a whole.

Since marrying Anita, I have been blessed with two sets of exceptional parents, Adela and Luis Ash *z"l* and Rosalie and Teddy (Tobias) Berman. They have cared for me, loved me, and modeled for me what it means to live a life of values.

I opened and close this book with words of profound gratitude to my heart and my life, Anita, and to my children, who are the most precious gift I have ever received from Hashem.

I save my last expression of gratitude for *Hakadosh Baruch Hu*. I aspire to feel the words of *Modeh Ani* all day long.

References

PAGE 1

Rava said: After departing from this world – Shabbat 31a:

אָמַר רָבָא: בְּשָׁעָה שֶׁמַּכְנִיסִין אָדָם לְדִין, אוֹמְרִים לוֹ: נָשָׂאתָ וְנָתַתָּ בֶּאֱמוּנָה? קָבַעְתָּ עִתִּים לַתּוֹרָה? עָסַקְתָּ בִּפְרִיָּה וּרְבִיָּה? צִפִּיתָ לִישׁוּעָה? פִּלְפַּלְתָּ בְּחָכְמָה? הֵבַנְתָּ דָּבָר מִתּוֹךְ דָּבָר?

Rava said: After departing from this world, when a person is brought to judgment for the life he lived in this world, they say to him: Did you conduct business faithfully? Did you designate times for Torah study? Did you engage in procreation? Did you anticipate the redemption? Did you engage in the dialectics of wisdom? Did you understand one matter from another?

PAGE 14

At times "not during night or day" – Menachot 99b:

שָׁאַל בֶּן דָּמָה בֶּן אֲחוֹתוֹ שֶׁל רַבִּי יִשְׁמָעֵאל אֶת רַבִּי יִשְׁמָעֵאל: כְּגוֹן אֲנִי, שֶׁלָּמַדְתִּי כָּל הַתּוֹרָה כּוּלָּהּ, מַהוּ לִלְמוֹד חָכְמַת יְוָנִית? קָרָא

131

עָלָיו הַמִּקְרָא הַזֶּה "לֹא יָמוּשׁ סֵפֶר הַתּוֹרָה הַזֶּה מִפִּיךָ וְהָגִיתָ בּוֹ יוֹמָם וָלַיְלָה", צֵא וּבְדוֹק שָׁעָה שֶׁאֵינָה לֹא מִן הַיּוֹם וְלֹא מִן הַלַּיְלָה, וּלְמוֹד בָּהּ חָכְמַת יְוָנִית.

Ben Dama, son of Rabbi Yishmael's sister, asked Rabbi Yishmael: In the case of one such as I, who has learned the entire Torah, what is the *Halacha* with regard to studying Greek wisdom? Rabbi Yishmael recited this verse about him: "This Torah scroll shall not depart from your mouth, and you shall contemplate it day and night." Go and search for an hour that is neither part of the day nor part of the night and learn Greek wisdom in it.

PAGE 15

She moved about in a mental cloud – Hardy, Thomas. *Tess of the D'Urbervilles.* Penguin Classics, 2003, p. 212.

PAGE 22

The first midrash *in* Bereshit Rabba (1:1):

הַתּוֹרָה אוֹמֶרֶת אֲנִי הָיִיתִי כְּלִי אֻמָּנוּתוֹ שֶׁל הַקָּדוֹשׁ בָּרוּךְ הוּא, בְּנֹהַג שֶׁבָּעוֹלָם מֶלֶךְ בָּשָׂר וָדָם בּוֹנֶה פָּלָטִין, אֵינוֹ בּוֹנֶה אוֹתָהּ מִדַּעַת עַצְמוֹ אֶלָּא מִדַּעַת אֻמָּן, וְהָאֻמָּן אֵינוֹ בּוֹנֶה אוֹתָהּ מִדַּעַת עַצְמוֹ אֶלָּא דִּפְתְּרָאוֹת וּפִנְקְסָאוֹת יֵשׁ לוֹ, לָדַעַת הֵיאךְ הוּא עוֹשֶׂה חֲדָרִים, הֵיאךְ הוּא עוֹשֶׂה פִּשְׁפְּשִׁין. כָּךְ הָיָה הַקָּדוֹשׁ בָּרוּךְ הוּא מַבִּיט בַּתּוֹרָה וּבוֹרֵא אֶת הָעוֹלָם, וְהַתּוֹרָה אָמְרָה בְּרֵאשִׁית בָּרָא אֱלֹהִים. וְאֵין רֵאשִׁית אֶלָּא תוֹרָה, הֵיאךְ מָה דְאַתְּ אָמַר (משלי ח, כב): ה' קָנָנִי רֵאשִׁית דַּרְכּוֹ.

In the way of the world, a king of flesh and blood who builds a castle does not do so based on his own knowledge, but rather based on the knowledge of an architect, and the architect does not build it based on his own knowledge, but rather has scrolls and books in order to know how to make rooms and doorways. Similarly, Hashem gazed into the

Torah and created the world. The Torah states, "Through the *reishit* Hashem created [the heavens and the earth]," and *reishit* means Torah, as in the verse "Hashem made me [the Torah] the beginning [*reishit*] of His way" (*Mishlei* 8:22).

The awful thing is that – Dostoyevsky, Fyodor. *The Brothers Karamazov*. Translated by David McDuff. Penguin Classics, 2003, p. 757.

PAGE 23

Viktor Frankl would later regard as the basis for logotherapy in Man's Search for Meaning – Frankl, Viktor E. *Man's Search for Meaning: An Introduction to Logotherapy*. Beacon Press, 2006.

PAGE 24

Yeshiva aims at unity – "Memorial Services Honor Dr. Dov Revel." *The Commentator*, Yeshiva University (Dec. 2, 1965).

https://repository.yu.edu/bitstream/handle/20.500.12202/5449/YUL.Commentator.5.1965-12-02.IXII.04.pdf?sequence=1

PAGE 25

The Lonely Man of Faith – Soloveitchik, Joseph B. *The Lonely Man of Faith*. Maggid Books, 2006, chapter 1.

PAGE 31

Torah Umadda – Lamm, Norman. *Torah Umadda: The Encounter of Religious Learning and Worldly Knowledge in the Jewish Tradition*. Maggid Books, 2010.

I have experienced a lifelong romance – Ibid., p. xii.

The big void in my education – Ibid., p. 200.

PAGE 34

Few matters concern us – Lichtenstein, Aharon. *Leaves of Faith: The World of Jewish Learning*, vol. 1. Ktav Publishing House, 2003, p. 89.

We cannot combat worldliness – Ibid., p. 92.

Be diligent in the study of the Torah – Avot 2:19:

רַבִּי אֶלְעָזָר אוֹמֵר, הֱוֵי שָׁקוּד לִלְמֹד תּוֹרָה, וְדַע מַה שֶּׁתָּשִׁיב לְאֶפִּיקוֹרוֹס. וְדַע לִפְנֵי מִי אַתָּה עָמֵל. וְנֶאֱמָן הוּא בַּעַל מְלַאכְתֶּךָ שֶׁיְּשַׁלֶּם לְךָ שְׂכַר פְּעֻלָּתֶךָ·

Rabbi Elazar said: Be diligent in the study of the Torah, and know how to answer a heretic; and know before whom you toil and that your employer is faithful, for He will pay you the reward of your labor.

PAGE 35

Not only helpful but indispensable – Lichtenstein, Aharon. "A Consideration of Synthesis." Op cit., p. 93.

At the very least heksher talmud Torah – Ibid.

Rambam's well-known adage – Introduction to *Avot* (The Eight Chapters):

וּבְמַה שֶּׁיָּבֹא מִן הַפֵּרוּשׁ אֵינָם עִנְיָנִים בְּדִיתִים אֲנִי מֵעַצְמִי, וְלֹא פֵּרוּשִׁים שֶׁחִדַּשְׁתִּים, וְאָמְנָם הֵם עִנְיָנִים לְקַטְתִּים מִדִּבְרֵי הַחֲכָמִים בַּמִּדְרָשׁוֹת וּבַתַּלְמוּד וְזוּלָתוֹ מֵחִבּוּרֵיהֶם, וּמִדִּבְרֵי הַפִילוֹסוֹפִים גַּם כֵּן הַקְּדוּמִים וְהַחֲדָשִׁים, וּמֵחִבּוּרִים הַרְבֵּה מִבְּנֵי אָדָם, וּשְׁמַע הָאֱמֶת מִמִּי שֶׁאֲמָרָהּ.

I have gleaned them from the words of the wise occurring in the *Midrashim*, in the Talmud, and in other of their works, as well as from the words of the philosophers, ancient and recent, and also from the works of various authors, as one should accept the truth from whoever states it.

PAGE 36

Commitment is the permanent recognition – Lichtenstein, Aharon. Op cit., p. 102.

PAGE 44

Positive freedom – Berlin, Isaiah. *Two Concepts of Liberty: An Inaugural Lecture Delivered Before the University of Oxford.* Clarendon Press, 1958, p. 23.

We know that people can maintain – Kahneman, Daniel. *Thinking, Fast and Slow.* Farrar, Straus and Giroux, 2011, p. 217.

PAGE 45

As the Zohar teaches – Zohar, Parshat Vayishlach, 60.

קֻדְשָׁא בְּרִיךְ הוּא תּוֹרָה אִיקְרֵי.

The Holy One, blessed be He, is called the Torah.

For Rabbi Soloveitchik, the ideal "Halakhic Man" internalizes – Soloveitchik, Joseph B. *Halakhic Man.* Jewish Publication Society, 1991.

PAGE 46

As Rambam writes – Hilchot Yesodei Ha-Torah 2:2:

וְהֵיאַךְ הִיא הַדֶּרֶךְ לְאַהֲבָתוֹ וְיִרְאָתוֹ. בְּשָׁעָה שֶׁיִּתְבּוֹנֵן הָאָדָם בְּמַעֲשָׂיו וּבְרוּאָיו הַנִּפְלָאִים הַגְּדוֹלִים וְיִרְאֶה מֵהֶן חָכְמָתוֹ שֶׁאֵין לָה עֵרֶךְ וְלֹא קֵץ מִיָּד הוּא אוֹהֵב וּמְשַׁבֵּחַ וּמְפָאֵר וּמִתְאַוֶּה תַּאֲוָה גְדוֹלָה לֵידַע הַשֵּׁם הַגָּדוֹל.

What is the path [to attain] love and fear of Him? When a person contemplates His wondrous and great deeds and creations and appreciates His infinite wisdom that surpasses all comparison, he will immediately love, praise, and glorify [Him], yearning with tremendous desire to know [God's] great name.

PAGE 49

The Talmud teaches that – Yoma 69b:

אָמַר רַב חֲנִינָא: שְׁמַע מִינַּה חוֹתָמוֹ שֶׁל הַקָּדוֹשׁ בָּרוּךְ הוּא אֱמֶת.

Rav Chanina said: Learn from this that the seal of the Holy One, blessed be He, is truth.

PAGE 50

God judges unfavorably those who lie, because they enhance falsehood and diminish the Divine in our world – Sota 42a:

אָמַר רַבִּי יִרְמְיָה בַּר אַבָּא אַרְבַּע כִּיתּוֹת אֵין מְקַבְּלוֹת פְּנֵי שְׁכִינָה כַּת לֵיצִים וְכַת חֲנֵיפִים וְכַת שַׁקָּרִים וְכַת מְסַפְּרֵי לָשׁוֹן הָרָע.

Rabbi Yirmeya bar Abba says: Four classes of people will not greet the divine presence: The class of cynics, and the class of flatterers, and the class of liars, and the class of slanderers.

PAGE 55

This is confirmed in a Mishna that likens Hashem's work to that of a craftsman – Sanhedrin 4:5:

שֶׁאָדָם טוֹבֵעַ כַּמָּה מַטְבְּעוֹת בְּחוֹתָם אֶחָד וְכֻלָּן דּוֹמִין זֶה לָזֶה, וּמֶלֶךְ מַלְכֵי הַמְּלָכִים הַקָּדוֹשׁ בָּרוּךְ הוּא טָבַע כָּל אָדָם בְּחוֹתָמוֹ שֶׁל אָדָם הָרִאשׁוֹן וְאֵין אֶחָד מֵהֶן דּוֹמֶה לַחֲבֵרוֹ. לְפִיכָךְ כָּל אֶחָד וְאֶחָד חַיָּב לוֹמַר, בִּשְׁבִילִי נִבְרָא הָעוֹלָם.

When a person stamps several coins with one seal, they are all similar to one another. But the supreme King of kings, the Holy One, blessed be He, stamped all people with the seal of Adam, the first human, [as all of them are his offspring,] yet not one of them is similar to another. Therefore, [since all humanity descends from one person,] each and every person is obligated to say: "The world was created for me."

PAGE 57

"Bowling alone" – Putnam, Robert D. *Bowling Alone: The Collapse and Revival of American Community.* Simon & Schuster, 2000.

PAGE 58

In The Dignity of Difference – Sacks, Jonathan. *The Dignity of Difference: How to Avoid the Clash of Civilizations.* Bloomsbury Continuum, 2003, p. 72.

"If I am not for myself, who will be for me?" – *Avot* 1:14:

הוּא הָיָה אוֹמֵר - אִם אֵין אֲנִי לִי, מִי לִי, וּכְשֶׁאֲנִי לְעַצְמִי, מָה אֲנִי.
וְאִם לֹא עַכְשָׁיו, אֵימָתַי.

He used to say: If I am not for myself, who will be for me? And if I am only for myself, what am I? And if not now, when?

PAGE 59

The movie Chariots of Fire, *which was released in 1981* – Hudson, Hugh, Colin Welland, and David Puttnam. *Chariots of Fire.* Enigma Productions, 1981.

PAGE 61

I may have very few good traits – Rakeffet-Rothkoff, Aaron. *The Rav: The World of Rabbi Joseph B. Soloveitchik*, vol. 2. Ktav Publishing House, 1999, pp. 225–226.

PAGE 62

I knew that I would lose my originality if I tried to be what I was not – Ibid., p. 226.

This school is unique – Ibid., p. 227.

PAGE 65

As articulated by Rabbi Soloveitchik – Soloveitchik, Joseph B. *Worship of the Heart: Essays on Jewish Prayer*. Ktav Publishing House, 2003.

It is fundamentally a service of the heart – Ta'anit 2a:

וּמְנָא לָן דִּבְתְפִלָּה - דְּתַנְיָא: "לְאַהֲבָה אֶת ה' אֱלֹהֵיכֶם וּלְעָבְדוֹ
בְּכָל לְבַבְכֶם": אֵיזוֹ הִיא עֲבוֹדָה שֶׁהִיא בַּלֵּב, הֱוֵי אוֹמֵר: זוֹ תְּפִלָּה.

And from where do we derive [that rain must be mentioned specifically] in the *Amida*? As it was taught in a *baraita* [with regard to the verse] "To love the Lord your God and to serve Him with all your heart" (*Devarim* 11:13). What can be described as service of the heart? Prayer.

PAGE 66

I am lonely – Soloveitchik, Joseph B. *Lonely Man of Faith*, p. 3.

PAGE 67

The flight of the alone to the alone – Plotinus, *The Enneads*. Translated by S. Mackenena. Larson Publications, 1992, p. 709.

Rambam maintains that the obligation to pray daily is from the Torah – Hilchot Tefilla (Laws of Prayer 1:1):

מִצְוַת עֲשֵׂה לְהִתְפַּלֵּל בְּכָל יוֹם שֶׁנֶּאֱמַר "וַעֲבַדְתֶּם אֵת ה' אֱלֹהֵיכֶם".
מִפִּי הַשְּׁמוּעָה לָמְדוּ שֶׁעֲבוֹדָה זוֹ הִיא תְּפִלָּה שֶׁנֶּאֱמַר "וּלְעָבְדוֹ בְּכָל
לְבַבְכֶם" אָמְרוּ חֲכָמִים אֵי זוֹ הִיא עֲבוֹדָה שֶׁבַּלֵּב זוֹ תְּפִלָּה. וְאֵין

מִנְיַן הַתְּפִלּוֹת מִן הַתּוֹרָה. וְאֵין מִשְׁנֵה הַתְּפִלָּה הַזֹּאת מִן הַתּוֹרָה. וְאֵין לַתְּפִלָּה זְמַן קָבוּעַ מִן הַתּוֹרָה.

It is a positive commandment to pray each day, as the verse states, "And you shall serve Hashem, your God." The Sages learned that this service is prayer, as the verse states, "And to serve Him with all your heart" (*Devarim* 11:13), on which the Sages commented, "What may be described as service of the heart? Prayer." The number of prayers is not prescribed in the Torah, and the form of prayer is not prescribed in the Torah, nor does the Torah prescribe a fixed time for prayer.

Ramban (Nahmanides), in his gloss to the Sefer Ha-Mitzvot – Positive Mitzva 5):

אֶלָּא וַדַּאי כָּל עִנְיַן הַתְּפִלָּה אֵינוּ חוֹבָה כְּלָל אֲבָל הוּא מִמִּדַּת חֶסֶד הַבּוֹרֵא יִתְבָּרַךְ עָלֵינוּ שֶׁשּׁוֹמֵעַ וְעוֹנֶה בְּכָל קָרְאֵנוּ אֵלָיו, וְעִקַּר הַכָּתוּב וּלְעָבְדוֹ בְּכָל לְבַבְכֶם מִצְוַת עֲשֵׂה שֶׁתִּהְיֶה כָּל עֲבוֹדָתֵנוּ לָאֵל יִתְעַלֶּה בְּכָל לְבָבֵנוּ כְּלוֹמַר בְּכַוָּנָה רְצוּיָה שְׁלֵמָה לִשְׁמוֹ וּבְאֵין הִרְהוּר רַע, לֹא שֶׁנַּעֲשֶׂה הַמִּצְוֹת בְּלִי כַּוָּנָה אוֹ עַל הַסָּפֵק אוּלַי יֵשׁ בָּהֶם תּוֹעֶלֶת, כְּעִנְיָן וְאָהַבְתָּ אֵת ה' אֱלֹהֶיךָ בְּכָל לְבָבְךָ וּבְכָל נַפְשְׁךָ וּבְכָל מְאֹדֶךָ שֶׁהַמִּצְוָה הִיא לֶאֱהֹב אֶת הַשֵּׁם בְּכָל לֵב וְלֵב וְשֶׁנִּסְתַּכֵּן בְּאַהֲבָתוֹ בְּנַפְשֵׁנוּ וּבְמָמוֹנֵנוּ. וּמַה שֶּׁדָּרְשׁוּ בְּסִפְרֵי וּלְעָבְדוֹ זֶה תַּלְמוּד, ד"א זוֹ תְּפִלָּה אַסְמַכְתָּא הִיא אוֹ לוֹמַר שֶׁמִּכְּלַל הָעֲבוֹדָה שֶׁנִּלְמַד תּוֹרָתוֹ וְשֶׁנִּתְפַּלֵּל אֵלָיו בְּעֵת הַצָּרוֹת.

But the concept of prayer is certainly not obligatory at all; rather, it is a kindness from the Blessed Creator, who listens and answers whenever we call on Him. Whereas the main meaning of the text "and to serve Him with all your heart" is the positive commandment that all our worship of God shall be with all our hearts – that is, with positive and full intention and without harmful doubt; that we should perform the commandments without intention or with doubt as to whether they have any benefit, just as "Love the Lord your God with all your heart, with all your soul, and with all your might" is the commandment of loving God with a whole heart – even risking our lives and possessions for His love. But the explanation in the Sifri that "and to serve Him" refers explicitly...to prayer [is incorrect; it] is either an *asmakhta*, or just an example of serving God, which includes studying Torah and praying to Him in times of trouble.

PAGE 68

Prayer is a mode of expression – Soloveitchik, Joseph B. *Worship of the Heart*, p. 3.

Prayer is the tale of an aching and yearning heart – Ibid., p. 20.

PAGE 70

The Gemara teaches us – Bava Kama 92a:

> כָּל הַמְבַקֵּשׁ רַחֲמִים עַל חֲבֵירוֹ וְהוּא צָרִיךְ לְאוֹתוֹ דָּבָר, הוּא נַעֲנָה תְּחִילָה? אֲמַר לֵיהּ, דִּכְתִיב: "וַה' שָׁב אֶת שְׁבוּת אִיּוֹב בְּהִתְפַּלְלוֹ בְּעַד רֵעֵהוּ".

Anyone who asks for compassion from Heaven on behalf of another, and he requires compassion from Heaven concerning that same matter, he is answered first. [Rabba bar Mari] said to him [that the source for this is] as it is written: "And Hashem changed the fortune of Iyov, when he prayed for his friends" (*Iyov* 42:10).

The Gemara illustrates different ways that the Amora'im, *the talmudic Sages, would prepare for prayer* – Shabbat 10b:

> "הִכּוֹן לִקְרַאת אֱלֹהֶיךָ יִשְׂרָאֵל". רָבָא בַּר רַב הוּנָא רָמֵי פּוּזְמְקֵי וּמְצַלֵּי, אָמַר: "הִכּוֹן לִקְרַאת" וְגוֹ'. רָבָא שָׁדֵי גְּלִימֵיהּ וּפָכַר יְדֵיהּ

וּמְצַלֵּי. אֲמַר: "כְּעַבְדָּא קַמֵּיהּ מָרֵיהּ". אֲמַר רַב אָשֵׁי: חֲזֵינָא לֵיהּ
לְרַב כָּהֲנָא כִּי אִיכָּא צַעֲרָא בְּעָלְמָא, שָׁדֵי גְּלִימֵיהּ וּפָכַר יְדֵיהּ
וּמְצַלֵּי. אֲמַר: "כְּעַבְדָּא קַמֵּי מָרֵיהּ". כִּי אִיכָּא שְׁלָמָא לָבֵישׁ וּמִתְכַּסֵּי
וּמִתְעַטֵּף וּמְצַלֵּי. אֲמַר: "הִכּוֹן לִקְרַאת אֱלֹהֶיךָ יִשְׂרָאֵל".

"Prepare to greet your God, Israel" (*Amos* 4:12). Rava bar Rav
Huna would don expensive socks and pray, and he said he
would do this because it is written: "Prepare to greet your
God, Israel." Rava would not do so; rather, in his prayer he
would remove his cloak and clasp his hands and pray as a
slave before his master. Rav Ashi said: I saw that Rav Kahana, when there was suffering in the world, would remove
his cloak and clasp his hands and pray, as a slave before
his master. When there was peace in the world, he would
dress, and cover himself, and wrap himself in a significant
garment, and pray, and he said that he did so in fulfillment
of the verse "Prepare to greet your God, Israel."

PAGE 73

One of the Talmud's most famous debates – Berachot 35b:

תָּנוּ רַבָּנַן: "וְאָסַפְתָּ דְגָנֶךָ" מָה תַּלְמוּד לוֹמַר? – לְפִי שֶׁנֶּאֱמַר:
"לֹא יָמוּשׁ סֵפֶר הַתּוֹרָה הַזֶּה מִפִּיךָ" – יָכוֹל דְּבָרִים כִּכְתָבָן תַּלְמוּד
לוֹמַר: "וְאָסַפְתָּ דְגָנֶךָ" – הַנְהֵג בָּהֶן מִנְהַג דֶּרֶךְ אֶרֶץ, דִּבְרֵי רַבִּי
יִשְׁמָעֵאל.

רַבִּי שִׁמְעוֹן בֶּן יוֹחַאי אוֹמֵר: אֶפְשָׁר אָדָם חוֹרֵשׁ בִּשְׁעַת חֲרִישָׁה,
וְזוֹרֵעַ בִּשְׁעַת זְרִיעָה, וְקוֹצֵר בִּשְׁעַת קְצִירָה, וְדָשׁ בִּשְׁעַת דִּישָׁה,
וְזוֹרֶה בִּשְׁעַת הָרוּחַ, תּוֹרָה מַה תְּהֵא עָלֶיהָ.

The Sages taught: What is the meaning of that which the
verse states: "And you shall gather your grain"? Because it is
stated: "This Torah shall not depart from your mouths, and
you shall contemplate in it day and night" (*Yehoshua* 1:8), I
might have thought that these matters are to be understood

as they are written [i.e., one is to literally spend his days immersed exclusively in Torah study]. Therefore, the verse states: "And you shall gather your grain, your wine, and your oil" – assume in their regard the way of the world [i.e., set aside time not only for Torah, but also for work]. This is the statement of Rabbi Yishmael.

Rabbi Shimon ben Yochai says: Is it possible that a person plows in the plowing season and sows in the sowing season and harvests in the harvest season and threshes in the threshing season and winnows in the windy season, and is constantly busy? What will become of Torah?

PAGE 75

Rashi, quoting Chazal, teaches that lasuach *means that Yitzchak was "praying" in the field* – Rashi, Bereshit 24:63, s.v. lasuach:

לְשׁוֹן תְּפִלָּה (בראשית רבה), כְּמוֹ יִשְׁפֹּךְ שִׂיחוֹ (תהילים קב):

This means "to pray" (*Bereshit Rabba* 60:14), as we find in the verse (*Tehillim* 102:1), "When he pours forth his complaint."

Chazal *teach us that this verse is the source for* tefillat Mincha, *the afternoon prayer* – Berachot 26b:

יִצְחָק תִּקֵּן תְּפִלַּת מִנְחָה, שֶׁנֶּאֱמַר "וַיֵּצֵא יִצְחָק לָשׂוּחַ בַּשָּׂדֶה לִפְנוֹת עֶרֶב", וְאֵין "שִׂיחָה" אֶלָּא תְּפִלָּה, שֶׁנֶּאֱמַר "תְּפִלָּה לְעָנִי כִי יַעֲטֹף וְלִפְנֵי ה' יִשְׁפֹּךְ שִׂיחוֹ".

Yitzchak instituted the afternoon prayer, as it is stated: "And Yitzchak went out to converse [*lasuach*] in the field toward evening" (*Bereshit* 24:63), and conversation means nothing other than prayer, as it is stated: "A prayer of the afflicted when he is faint and pours out his complaint [*sicho*] before Hashem" (*Tehillim* 102:1).

Rabbi Shmuel ben Meir (Rashbam), Rashi's grandson, teaches that the literal reading of the word lasuach *is "to plant"* – Rashbam, *Bereshit* 24:63:

כְּדִכְתִיב: וְכָל שִׂיחַ הַשָּׂדֶה כְּלוֹמַר: לָטַעַת אִילָנוֹת וְלִרְאוֹת עִנְיְנֵי פּוֹעֲלָיו וְאָז בִּהְיוֹתוֹ בַּשָּׂדֶה רָאָה גְּמַלִּים בָּאִים וְהָלַךְ לִקְרָאתָם לִרְאוֹת אִם הֵם גְּמַלֵּי אָבִיו שֶׁהוֹלִיךְ הָעֶבֶד.

[The word לָשׂוּחַ should be understood] in the manner of the verse שִׂיחַ הַשָּׂדֶה, "the plants that grow in the field" (*Bereshit* 2:5). In other words, [Yitzchak went out] to plant trees and to oversee the work of his employees. While he was thus occupied in the field, he happened to espy camels approaching, and he came closer to see if perchance they were the camels belonging to his father that the servant had been leading.

PAGE 76

Rabbi Yitzchak Hutner was once asked for advice – Hutner, Yitzchak. *Pachad Yitzchak, Iggrot U-Michtavim.* Mossad Gur Aryeh, letter 94.

PAGE 77

The Talmud teaches that the command to love Hashem is also a command to make the name of Hashem more beloved in the world – Yoma 86a:

"וְאָהַבְתָּ אֵת ה' אֱלֹהֶיךָ", שֶׁיְּהֵא שֵׁם שָׁמַיִם מִתְאַהֵב עַל יָדְךָ. שֶׁיְּהֵא קוֹרֵא וְשׁוֹנֶה וּמְשַׁמֵּשׁ תַּלְמִידֵי חֲכָמִים, וִיהֵא מַשָּׂאוֹ וּמַתָּנוֹ בְּנַחַת עִם הַבְּרִיּוֹת, מָה הַבְּרִיּוֹת אוֹמְרוֹת עָלָיו - אַשְׁרֵי אָבִיו שֶׁלִּמְּדוֹ תּוֹרָה, אַשְׁרֵי רַבּוֹ שֶׁלִּמְּדוֹ תּוֹרָה. אוֹי לָהֶם לַבְּרִיּוֹת שֶׁלֹּא לָמְדוּ תּוֹרָה, פְּלוֹנִי שֶׁלִּמְּדוֹ תּוֹרָה - רְאוּ כַּמָּה נָאִים דְּרָכָיו, כַּמָּה מְתֻקָּנִים מַעֲשָׂיו. עָלָיו הַכָּתוּב אוֹמֵר: "וַיֹּאמֶר לִי עַבְדִּי אָתָּה יִשְׂרָאֵל אֲשֶׁר בְּךָ אֶתְפָּאָר".

"And you shall love the Lord your God" (*Devarim* 6:5) – this means that you should make the name of Heaven beloved. [How should one do so?] He should read Torah, and learn Mishna, and serve Torah scholars, and he should be pleasant with people in his business transactions. What do people say about such a person? Fortunate is his father who taught him Torah! Fortunate is his teacher who taught him Torah! Woe to the people who have not studied Torah! So-and-so, who was taught Torah, see how pleasant are his ways, how proper are his deeds. The verse states about him and others like him: "You are My servant, Israel, in whom I will be glorified" (*Yeshayahu* 49:3).

PAGE 79

Rabbi Soloveitchik explained – Soloveitchik, Joseph B. *Shiurei Harav: A Conspectus of the Public Lectures of Rabbi Joseph B. Soloveitchik.* Edited by Joseph Epstein. Ktav Publishing House, 1994, pp. 103–104.

There is a midrash that praises Chanoch – see *Midrash Talpiot* under "Chanoch."

The Rav once said that if he could write a fourteenth Ani Ma'amin – Soloveitchik, Joseph B. *The Rav Speaks: Five Addresses on Israel, History, and the Jewish People.* Toras HoRav Foundation, 2002, pp. 174–178.

PAGE 80

One of the opinions in the Midrash is that the letter that marked Kayin's head after he killed his brother Hevel was a letter ו – *Tikunei Zohar, Tikun 69, p. 118b:*

וַיֹּאמֶר קַיִן אֶל ה' גָּדוֹל עֲוֹנִי מִנְּשׂוֹא, הָכָא תָב בִּתְיוּבְתָּא וְאִתְחֲרַט, בְּגִין דָא וַיָּשֶׂם ה' לְקַיִן אוֹת, הָכָא רָמַז אוֹת בְּרִית מִילָה דְקַבִּיל

יִתְרוֹ, דְּאִתְּמַר בֵּיהּ וּבְנֵי קֵנִי חֹתֵן מֹשֶׁה שֶׁנִּפְרַד מִקַּיִן, וּבְיִתְרוֹ
אִתְתַּקַן קַיִן מֵחוֹבֵיהּ, וְעוֹד דְּבַהַהוּא זִמְנָא קַבִּיל לֵיהּ, בְּגִין דְּאַחֲזֵי
לֵיהּ בְּנוֹי דְּקֵנֵי חֹתֵן מֹשֶׁה דַּהֲווֹ עֲתִידִין לְמֶהֱוֵי בְּלִשְׁכַּת הַגָּזִית,
אָמַר וְכִי לְחַיָּבָא קַבִּיל קוּדְשָׁא בְּרִיךְ הוּא בִּתְשׁוּבָה, עַל אַחַת כַּמָּה
וְכַמָּה לַצַּדִּיקַיָּיא, מִיָּד וַיֵּצֵא קַיִן מִלִּפְנֵי ה', בְּהַאי נָפַק מִן דִּינָא,
וְקַבִּיל עֲלֵיהּ כָּל מַה דְּאִתְגַּזַּר בֵּיהּ, דִּכְתִיב וַיֵּשֶׁב בְּאֶרֶץ נוֹד, מַה
דְּאָמַר לֵיהּ נָד, שַׁוִּי עֲלֵיהּ ו' וְאִתְעֲבִיד נוֹד, וְדָא אִיהוּ דְּאִתְּמַר בֵּיהּ
וַיָּשֶׂם ה' לְקַיִן אוֹת לְבִלְתִּי הַכּוֹת אוֹתוֹ, דְּאִם הֲוָה נָד אִתְּמַר בֵּיהּ
וְהָיָה כָל מוֹצְאִי יַהַרְגֵנִי, וּבְגִין דְּתָב בִּתְיוּבְתָּא וְקַבִּיל עֲלֵיהּ אוֹת
בְּרִית, שַׁוֵּי עֲלֵיהּ אוֹת ו' לְשֵׁזָבָא לֵיהּ, וְלָא עוֹד אֶלָּא דְּשַׁוֵּי לֵיהּ
קַדְמַת עֵדֶן, דִּבְגִינֵיהּ זָכָה לְגַן עֵדֶן.

PAGE 86

There is an additional element of love because Hashem makes known to us our special relationship with Him – Avot 3:14:

הוּא הָיָה אוֹמֵר, חָבִיב אָדָם שֶׁנִּבְרָא בְצֶלֶם. חִבָּה יְתֵרָה נוֹדַעַת לוֹ
שֶׁנִּבְרָא בְצֶלֶם, שֶׁנֶּאֱמַר (בראשית ט) כִּי בְּצֶלֶם אֱלֹהִים עָשָׂה אֶת
הָאָדָם.

He used to say: Beloved is man for he was created in the image [of God]. Especially beloved is he for it was made known to him that he had been created in the image [of God], as it is said: "For in the image of God He made man" (*Bereshit* 9:6).

As Rambam writes when codifying acts of kindness – Hilchot Avel 14:1–2:

מִצְוַת עֲשֵׂה שֶׁל דִּבְרֵיהֶם לְבַקֵּר חוֹלִים. וּלְנַחֵם אֲבֵלִים. וּלְהוֹצִיא
הַמֵּת. וּלְהַכְנִיס הַכַּלָּה. וּלְלַוּוֹת הָאוֹרְחִים... וְכֵן לְשַׂמֵּחַ הַכַּלָּה
וְהֶחָתָן. וּלְסַעֲדָם בְּכָל צָרְכֵיהֶם. וְאֵלּוּ הֵן גְּמִילוּת חֲסָדִים שֶׁבְּגוּפוֹ
שֶׁאֵין לָהֶם שִׁעוּר. אַף עַל פִּי שֶׁכָּל מִצְוֹת אֵלּוּ מִדִּבְרֵיהֶם הֲרֵי הֵן
בִּכְלַל (ויקרא יט, יח) "וְאָהַבְתָּ לְרֵעֲךָ כָּמוֹךָ". כָּל הַדְּבָרִים שֶׁאַתָּה

רוֹצֶה שֶׁיַּעֲשׂוּ אוֹתָם לְךָ אֲחֵרִים. עֲשֵׂה אַתָּה אוֹתָן לְאָחִיךָ בְּתוֹרָה
וּבְמִצְוֹת:

It is a rabbinic positive precept to visit the sick, comfort the mourners, escort the dead, dower the bride, accompany the [departing] guests…as well as to cheer the bride and the groom and to assist them in whatever they need. These constitute acts of kindness performed with one's body that have no limit. Even though all these precepts are of rabbinic origin, they are implied in the biblical verse "You shall love your neighbor as yourself" (*Vayikra* 19:18); that is, whatever you would have others do to you, do for your brothers in Torah and precepts.

PAGE 87

In Totality and Infinity – Levinas, Emmanuel. *Totality and Infinity: An Essay on Exteriority.* Translated by Alphonso Lingis. Duquesne University Press, 1969, p. 299.

In the face the Other – Ibid., p. 262.

PAGE 88

To borrow once again from the Rav's archetypes of Adam I and Adam II – Soloveitchik, Joseph B. *Lonely Man of Faith*, chapter 1.

PAGE 92

Rambam includes redemption as one of his thirteen principles of belief – Rambam, Introduction to *Sanhedrin*, chapter 10 (*Perek Chelek*).

PAGE 97

Knocking on the door of the Jewish people – Soloveitchik, Joseph B. "Six Knocks," in *Kol Dodi Dofek*. Translated by David Gordon. Ktav Publishing House, 2006.

PAGE 104

Rabbi Soloveitchik famously distinguished – Ibid., "The Covenant of Destiny."

PAGE 107

Cited in the name of Rabbi Chaim Soloveitchik – Zevin, Shlomo Yosef. *Ishim Ve-Shitot*. Kol Mevaser, 2007, pp. 51–52.

PAGE 108

Rabbi Saadia Gaon – Saadiah Gaon, *Emunot Ve-De'ot* (The Book of Beliefs and Opinions), Introduction:

> מִלָּה שֶׁיִּשְׁמָעֶנָּה הָאָדָם בְּשֵׁם אֶחָד מִן הַמַּכְחִישִׁים וְהִגִּיעָה אֶל לִבּוֹ וְתִמְחָצֵהוּ וְיַעֲמֹד כָּל יָמָיו בְּמַחֲצוֹ. וּבוֹא אוֹמֵר (משלי יח, ח) דִּבְרֵי נִרְגָּן כְּמִתְלַהֲמִים וְגוֹ', וְלֹא חָשַׁב כִּי אִם לֹא יָגֵן עַל עַצְמוֹ מֵהַחֹם וְהַקֹּר יְבִיאוּהוּ אֶל הַמָּוֶת.

Something someone heard in the name of one of the deniers may touch his heart and worried him and he is thus stuck in worry his entire life. Thus is it said, "The words of a grumbler are like blows, and they go down into the innermost parts of the body" (*Mishlei* 18:8). This individual does not consider that if he does not protect himself from cold and heat, he will die [and he must likewise guard himself intellectually against heresy].

PAGES 111

In an article on his reflections on "Peace and Truth" – Lamm, Norman. "Peace and Truth: Part-Time Opponents." Sermon, July 10, 1951.

PAGES 112

Hineni, as explained by Rashi – Rashi, *Bereshit* 22:1, s.v. *hineni*:

> הִנֵּנִי. כָּךְ הִיא עֲנִיָּתָם שֶׁל חֲסִידִים, לְשׁוֹן עֲנָוָה הוּא וּלְשׁוֹן זִמּוּן:

"Here I am": Such is the answer of the pious; it is an expression of meekness and readiness (*Midrash Tanchuma, Vayera* 22).

PAGE 115

There is no minimum or maximum measure – Mishna, *Pe'ah* 1:1:

אֵלּוּ דְבָרִים שֶׁאֵין לָהֶם שִׁעוּר. הַפֵּאָה, וְהַבִּכּוּרִים, וְהָרְאָיוֹן, וּגְמִילוּת
חֲסָדִים, וְתַלְמוּד תּוֹרָה. אֵלּוּ דְבָרִים שֶׁאָדָם אוֹכֵל פֵּרוֹתֵיהֶן בָּעוֹלָם
הַזֶּה וְהַקֶּרֶן קַיֶּמֶת לוֹ לָעוֹלָם הַבָּא. כִּבּוּד אָב וָאֵם, וּגְמִילוּת חֲסָדִים,
וַהֲבָאַת שָׁלוֹם בֵּין אָדָם לַחֲבֵרוֹ, וְתַלְמוּד תּוֹרָה כְּנֶגֶד כֻּלָּם:

These are the things that have no definite quantity: The corners [of the field], first-fruits, [the offerings brought] on appearing [at the Temple on the three pilgrimage festivals], the performance of righteous deeds, and the study of the Torah. These are the things of which a man enjoys the fruits in this world while the principal remains for him in the World to Come: Honoring one's father and mother, the performance of righteous deeds, and the making of peace between a person and his friend; and the study of the Torah is equal to them all.

Rambam explains that the mitzva – *Hilchot Avel* 14:1; see text in note to p. 86, quoted above.

PAGE 116

Make for yourself a rabbi and acquire for yourself a friend – *Avot* 1:6:

יְהוֹשֻׁעַ בֶּן פְּרַחְיָה וְנִתַּאי הָאַרְבֵּלִי קִבְּלוּ מֵהֶם. יְהוֹשֻׁעַ בֶּן פְּרַחְיָה
אוֹמֵר, עֲשֵׂה לְךָ רַב, וּקְנֵה לְךָ חָבֵר, וֶהֱוֵי דָן אֶת כָּל הָאָדָם לְכַף זְכוּת.

Yehoshua ben Perachya and Nittai the Arbeli received [the oral tradition] from them. Yehoshua ben Perachya used to say: Make for yourself a rabbi and acquire for yourself a friend, and judge all men with the scale weighted in their favor.

PAGE 121

"By formulating his own experiences in clear language, others may benefit from this self-revelation and enrich their own religious life" – Rakeffet-Rothkoff, Aaron. *The Rav: The World of Rabbi Joseph B. Soloveitchik.* Ktav Publishing House, 1999, p. 1.

PAGE 123

The mandate cited in the paragraph of Shema *to teach one's children refers also to one's students* – Sifrei, Devarim 6:7:

לְבָנֶיךָ - אֵלּוּ תַּלְמִידֶיךָ. וְכֵן אַתָּה מוֹצֵא בְּכָל מָקוֹם, שֶׁהַתַּלְמִידִים קְרוּיִים בָּנִים, שֶׁנֶּאֱמַר "בָּנִים אַתֶּם לַה' אֱלֹהֵיכֶם", וְאוֹמֵר (מלכים ב' ב, ג) "וַיֵּצְאוּ בְנֵי הַנְּבִיאִים", וְכִי בְּנֵי הַנְּבִיאִים הָיוּ? וַהֲלֹא תַלְמִידִים הָיוּ! - אֶלָּא מִכָּאן לְתַלְמִידִים שֶׁהֵם קְרוּיִם בָּנִים.

"To your sons": These are your disciples. And thus do you find in all places that disciples are called "sons," as the verse states (II *Melachim* 2:3): "And the sons of the prophets came forth." Now were they the sons of the prophets? Were they not disciples? This shows that disciples were called "sons."

PAGE 124

True joy, according to Rabbi Soloveitchik – Schachter, Hershel. *Nefesh HaRav: Torah from Rabbi Joseph B. Soloveitchik.* Reishis Yerushalayim, Jerusalem 5754/1994, p. 314 (Hebrew).

The fonts used in this book are from the Arno Family

Maggid Books
The best of contemporary Jewish thought from
Koren Publishers Jerusalem Ltd.